Read what these professionals say about *Stress Management—Does Anyone in Chicago Know About It?*

"David Nelson has written a stress management primer for the layman. It should prove helpful for almost anyone dealing with this ubiquitous syndrome."

        William R. White, M.D.
        Physician

"I found this book to be easily understood and a personally applicable stress management tool for my patients with chronic pain and industrial disabilities."

        Roger Iburg, P.T.
        Senior Physical Therapist

"Practical, easy-to-read reference on managing stress. Appropriate for patients and should be in every physical therapist's library."

        Paul D. Hughes, P.T.
        President
        Health Trends of Florida, Inc.

"Provides a simple, common-sense approach to stress reduction, useful to both professionals and the public. It should serve as a beginning reference to people wanting to make changes in their lifestyles. The writing style makes the book fun to read."

        Mark D. Stoff, P.T.; M.Ed.
        Director
        Stoff Rehabilitation Services, Inc.

"A useful book for healthcare professionals, patients, and the general public. Stress is a major threat to good health, and David Nelson has given an easy-to-read, armchair approach to reducing stress. He appeals to all personality types and defuses the standard excuses before the reader has a chance to say, 'Yeah, but. . . .' If it worked for me, it can work for anyone."

        Lisa Adams, P.T.
        Director of Marketing
        Holmes Regional Medical Center

Contents

PART ONE
MAJOR LIFESTYLE CHANGES

1 What Is Stress? 3
2 Our Two Choices 9
3 Reactions 15
4 Coping Methods 23
5 Worry and Guilt 39

PART TWO
DAILY STRESSORS

6 Self-Esteem/Activities/Laughter 45
7 Purging/Friendships/Nutrition 51

PART THREE
REDUCING STRESS AT WORK

8 Interviewing and Training 63
9 Evaluations/Rewards/Job Description 71

PART FOUR
RETIREMENT AND STRESS

10 Problems with Retirement 79
11 Solutions to Retirement Stress 89

PART ONE

Major Lifestyle Changes

1
What Is Stress?

Stress! That awful word conjures up feelings of pressure, tension, frustration, and pain—just to name a few. As a physical therapist, I have been using stress reduction techniques for 18 years to help my patients. And as a living, breathing being, I have practiced these on myself for the past eight years—finally. And they do work. I have also been teaching stress coping techniques to the general public for the past seven years. Members of my classes have come from all walks of life and every socioeconomic level. This is only fitting, as stress captures the attention of all mankind.

Stress is probably as common as back pain in America where eight out of ten people suffer at times. Stress can be short lasting or present for decades. It can maim. It can kill! Take a look at our lifestyles. Thirteen million Americans are alcoholics. There is drug abuse, child abuse, sex abuse, and food abuse. Two of our leading causes of death are related to or aggravated by stress—stroke and heart attacks.

Benjamin Franklin once said, "Little strokes fell great oaks." No matter how strong we think we are, we must listen to both the body and—more importantly—the mind. If someone chopped a piece out of a huge oak tree each day with a small axe, that tree would one day collapse. We sometimes think we are all powerful and that "it won't happen to me." But that thinking is wrong!

When asked, "What does stress mean to you?" I have heard all kinds of responses, from those mentioned above to feelings of inadequacy, aggravation, loss of temper, and tears. I've heard others define stress as: anything which places a demand on us; pressure on the outside which can affect us on the inside; normal wear and tear process; an adaptive response in which the body prepares for or adjusts to any change in equilibrium; or an automatic response to a change.

Stress, most simply put, is change. Whenever we encounter change, we experience stress. It applies to a single-celled animal and runs the gamut throughout the animal kingdom, including Man. Be it light or electrical stimulus in a laboratory affecting the simple form of life, or changes in weather affecting us, all organisms face stress. And guess what! We can run, but we can't hide. Stress will be with us forever. The only time we won't have stress is when we die. For as long as there are changes in our lives there will always be a certain amount of stress.

Whenever I listen to former students, I always hear comments like, "Boy, do I ever need this. I'm having just an awful time." Or, "I sure hope this helps me. My life is miserable." Naturally I hear the ever-present "ooohs" and "aaahs" about such a negative theme. But I always get everyone's attention by stating that stress is both negative and positive. We react much the same way to the positive as we do to the negative. Our bodies respond in similar fashion to a marriage and to a divorce, to a birth and to a death, to getting hired on a new job and to getting fired from the old one, or to receiving a raise or a demotion. Positive stress can aid us with daily challenges. Some people need this type of stress to perform. But after the project is over, they have to take time to relax and rejuvenate the body and mind, thus preparing for the next challenge. Positive stress can help us to focus, concentrate, and perform better. Large problems are made up of little ones, like a jigsaw; and if we take the time to properly analyze and pull the problem apart, we will find the little pieces easy to work with. I have also noticed that people respond to what they perceive as being the truth or fact, not necessarily what is actually the truth or fact. The major difference is that with the positive stressors we let go sooner and don't dwell on them as long. Do you remember the last time you interviewed for a job? How was you stomach that morning? How did you sleep the night before? Do you remember the trickles of sweat running down your side as the interviewer asked you questions about your work record or what you could do for his company?

And do you remember ever being fired from a job or laid off? Remember your stomach, the sweat, or lack of sleep that fateful night? Yes, we do respond much the same way to opposite circumstances. What an irony of life! Positive stress helps us to set goals, work more efficiently, plan for the future, and appreciate what we have. Positive stress is a guide, and we need it. Negative stress is the culprit which we need to monitor, recognize, and control. Distress is the harmful, unpleasant stress or pressure on us. It leaves invisible chemical scars on the body.

Throughout this book, I will be providing you with numerous tricks, hints, and techniques for coping with stress. Practice them faithfully and go slowly, and you certainly will feel better. The greater number of stressors or changes you have, the greater your risk for becoming ill. The following is a list of major stress producers in order from high to low impact on us. The greater number of these that you experience, the higher your risk of becoming sick as a result of stress. You may find such lists in any major Sunday newspaper covering this topic. Take a few moments and check all the events that happened to you in the last 12 months.

- Death of a spouse
- Quit alcohol or drugs (unsuccessful)
- Quit alcohol or drugs (successful)
- Divorce
- Marrriage separation
- Jail term
- Death in family
- Injury or illness
- Marriage
- Terminated at work
- Marital reconciliation
- Change in health of family member
- Pregnancy
- Sex problems
- Addition of family member
- Business readjustment
- Change of financial status

- Death of friend
- Change to alternate line of work
- Change in number of arguments with spouse
- Mortgage over $10,000
- Foreclosure of loan
- Change of responsibilities at work
- Child's leaving home
- Problems with in-laws
- Significant personal achievements
- Spouse starts or stops work
- Start or finish of school
- Change of living conditions
- Change in personal habits
- Problems with employer
- Change of work hours
- Change of residence
- Change of schools
- Change of recreation
- Change of church activities
- Change of social activities
- Mortgage under $10,000
- Change of sleeping habits
- Change of number of family get-togethers
- Change of eating habits
- Vacation
- Christmas
- Minor violations of the law

What you have just completed is an emotional stress test or screening. The items listed on the test are known as stressors. Remember how I asked you to check all the items that occurred within the past 12 months? Did you ever hear the phrase, "Time heals all wounds"? Well, guess what! That applies to us with stress as well. For instance, if you are trying to stop smoking (give up drugs or alcohol), there's good news because that tension from your program lasts only one year—as a general rule. The same holds true for all the others on the list as well. But remember, this is only a general screening. It doesn't necessarily mean you have no stress.

Points to remember

1. Stress is any change.
2. The more stressors we have, the higher our stress level.
3. Time heals all wounds.
4. Effects of stress can be temporary or present for decades.
5. Stress can be a factor in heart attacks and strokes.
6. Positive stress helps us to focus, concentrate, and perform better.
7. We respond to what we *perceive* as fact, not what is actual fact.

2
Our Two Choices

People have told me about all kinds of ways they react to stress. Remember, these are respectable citizens of a very fine community. When asked, "How do you react to stress?" I have heard the following: "I throw things;" "I pout and don't talk;" "I cuss and swear;" "I drink;" "I cry;" "I worry;" "I pray;" "I run;" "I clean my house;" "I eat." How do *you* react to stress?

There's a part of the body called the autonomic nervous system which regulates the internal functions of the body. It operates mainly by contracting or relaxing the smooth muscles of our internal organs, such as the urinary bladder, gastrointestinal tract, uterus, and blood vessels. Smooth muscles should not be confused with the other two types of muscles found in the body—striated and coronary. The autonomic nervous system also regulates the secretion of various glands and controls the heart.

The goal of stress management should be to find a state of homeostasis or equilibrium in our body, mind, and spirit. There are two parts to the autonomic system which are designed for just that purpose. These are called the sympathetic and the parasympathetic. An analogy is that one is like the brakes on our car; and the other, like the gas pedal. When we experience homeostasis, we have one foot on the gas and the other on the brake, going slowly and easily.

The center for these two systems is found in the brain. The sympathetic system is like the gas pedal. It causes us to "go fast." When activated in a stressful situation, it creates the following effects on us: Eyes become dilated; movement of food in the gut region is reduced, thereby reducing the digestive process; we sweat profusely; our heart rate increases, as does the vigor of contraction and amount of blood flow; blood flow to our muscles is increased; bronchi (or breathing passages) in our lungs become larger to accommodate more air; the liver releases large amounts of glucose or sugar; kidneys decrease their output; mental activity increases; blood pressure rises; blood flow to the kidneys and intestine is reduced; and our metabolism is increased by some 50%. Metabolism is the physical and chemical process needed to maintain life. In short, the sympathetic response is greatest when we feel threatened or in a state of distress.

The braking system of our body is the parasympathetic response. It has just the opposite reactions on us. Its goal is to keep everything calmed down. This system will lower the heart rate, reduce the force of the heart contraction, reduce the blood flow through the coronary vessels, and in general cause the heart to relax. It also increases digestion, reduces the size of bronchi in the lungs, and lowers blood pressure.

Because both of these are controlled in the brain, all responses are automatic. We cannot control them. Whenever we are in a dangerous situation such as almost getting hit by a car or being scared by a vicious dog or frightened by a practical joker, the sympathetic response is immediate and uncontrollable. We were born to survive. The body does what the brain tells it. And a funny thing is that the brain does what the mind tells it. History's greatest thinkers say so:

> "The fault, dear Brutus, is not in our stars, but in ourselves. . . ." —Shakespeare's *Julius Caesar*

> "Man is disturbed not by things but the views he takes of them." —Epictetus

> "For as he thinketh in his heart, so is he." —Proverbs 23:7

Now picture, if you will, a caveman a million years ago sitting in his cave early in the morning. His son is across the cave watching as Dad prepares to do battle for the day's meal. Well, it so happens that Dad is a worrisome person and is always tense before battle. He paces, stomps, kicks dirt, swears, and wants to be left alone. As he leaves the cave, he immediately confronts a huge saber-toothed tiger. The caveman has only two choices—attack or run back into the cave. If he just stands there he might get eaten. With both choices comes the activation of the sympathetic response. Let's say the caveman runs back into the cave, where he immediately fusses, fumes, and in general demonstrates negative behavior—even by caveman standards. This process is repeated day after day, year after year.

Now the son, who has been watching this behavior for years becomes old enough to fight for food. What type of behavior do you think he will demonstrate? And so it goes, generation after generation, all the way down to Modern Man.

Research has shown that abused children have a higher possibility of becoming abusers than those who were not abused. The same holds true for alcohol and possibly even drug and food abuse. We all face daily "tigers" in our lives. These "tigers" represent change or stressors. How we react to stress has much to do with how we were shown (taught) to handle adversity or problems. This is called our nurturing.

This is not parent-bashing, however, because it also has to do with "nature." Did you ever know a family that had several children raised in the same house by the same parents and all the children turned out to be honorable people except for one child? Did you ever wonder why? This is the "nature" part of it. It's just the way things are. Stress has a lot to do with both "nature" and "nurture."

Nature, or genetics, is better known as temperament. Nurture is better known as the personality. Some of us have temperaments requiring high energy and high stress levels to feel good, to feel as though we are doing a good job. These people are known as Type A personalities. The Type B personality requires much less stress and fewer changes to feel content. One is not better than the other. It's just the way we are. The personality or nurture, i.e., how we were raised, can modify our temperament but cannot change it.

Are you a Type A or Type B personality? Do you talk a lot and rapidly? Are you always thinking about something else and constantly planning for the future? Are you aggressive, having difficulty relaxing or sitting still? Do you always need to be doing something? So, you say you don't know—then ask your friends or relatives. Better yet, ask the people you work with. If their answer to the above question is yes, you are probably a Type A personality. This is also known as the "racehorse."

Are you laid back? Do you like things quiet and simple? Is your idea of a vacation visiting museums or lying on the beach? Do your friends sometimes ask, "Doesn't anything ever bother you?" Then you probably are a Type B personality.

Have you ever said, "If one more thing happens, I'll scream!" or, "That's the straw that broke the camel's back"? And what about, "I'm so mad I can't see straight"? Two things occur when we think, or worse yet, say these things. First of all, we are saying to ourselves that we are under a lot of stress, and secondly, that we have crossed the line. We have exceeded our comfortable stress level and it's time to back up and re-group. Many patients come to me, and I ask if they are having a good day. With gritted teeth, clenched fists, and tightened facial muscles they say, "Why, sure." If you wonder if you are under too much stress, and if you ever find yourself saying any of the above statements, then you indeed are under a lot of pressure and it's time to act.

We all have those points where if one more thing happens we'll scream. That is our stress point or breaking point. Imagine for a moment a line representing an arbitrary amount of stress. To the left of the line at point zero is prebirth and to the far right of the line is death. Beyond these points is the only time we encounter no stress. Depending on your personality, you can find a point where you function best, where you "feel good." For Type A personalities, that point is more to the far right; for Type B personalities it is more to the left. Look at the diagram on the next page. Observe what happens when you don't have enough stress in your life, when you don't have enough change. In that state, you'll find boredom, depression, burn-out, and a feeling of being unmotivated. Look to the far right of the point on the diagram. Observe what happens when you have too many changes or too much stress. There you'll find anxiety, frustration, a sense of tension, and yes, burn-out.

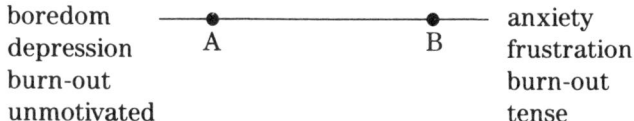

boredom			anxiety
depression	A	B	frustration
burn-out			burn-out
unmotivated			tense

Did you ever have a day at work when things were very slow and the day seemed to drag? There were no changes to speak of and therefore no real stress. How did you feel? Were you bored, depressed, unmotivated? I know in my business when things are slow we all become lazy. We all put things off—and, you know, those are the times we make most of our mistakes. Oh, that paperwork can wait till later; I'll send that report in later, and so on. We all feel blah.

On the other hand—how do you feel when things are absolutely chaotic? There aren't enough hours in a day. And when you are the most busy is when the unexpected happens. Every time you turn around something is going wrong. It is one of those days where Murphy's Law is working at its peak. Just ask an accountant about the feeling during tax season. Better yet, ask a working mother at any time. Both will shake their heads in agreement.

Several years ago, I volunteered my services to many nonprofit organizations in our community. This was in addition to building my practice. I was starting my day at 4 a.m. and ending at 10 p.m. Yes, I'll confess—I was a workaholic. I was burning my candle at both ends. I was at the point where if one more thing happened I would scream. Well, the unexpected happened. I had not one but two major family tragedies in a very short span of time. One day I crossed the line and said, "That's it—I quit. Enough is enough!" I called all the volunteer groups and resigned. I was a perfectionist, which made resigning all the more difficult. But guess what? As I contacted each group and quit, I felt better and better. I was purposely and consciously taking myself back below my stress point. And I felt great! I was living a sacred rule of stress management—do fewer things and do them better! This is a rule I learned from the school of hard knocks, and it has worked well for me ever since. Now I volunteer for only one organization and refuse to let myself get strung out. Stress management is a selfish program. You must be willing to make a commitment to yourself.

Another thing to remember is that you will never graduate. You will never finish. There will always be stress. There will always be changes.

Points to remember

1. The goal of stress management is to find a state of equilibrium.
2. Reaction to stress comes from both nurture and nature.
3. Our body's reaction is from the nervous system, and we can't control it once it starts—it's automatic. We can't prevent the reaction, but we can prevent it from starting in the first place.
4. Are you a Type A or Type B personality?
5. Too little or too much stress can create problems for us.
6. Do fewer things, and do them better.
7. The fault is not in our stars but in ourselves.

3
Reactions

Remember that caveman who encountered his morning stress or change—that mean, old, nasty saber-toothed tiger? The caveman had two choices to make. He could have attacked or he could have run away. Imagine Modern Man. Suppose you encounter a Pit Bull dog or a Doberman snarling and growling in your face, wanting nothing better than to attack you. What choices do you have? Or better yet, suppose you encounter your boss at the door one day and he is growling and snarling. What two choices do you have? In both situations, your choice is fight or flight. You can attack, or you can run away. There are times when to fight is not socially acceptable, and you have to run away. In the case of the boss, it's obviously more prudent to stuff your feelings temporarily and meet with him later. In the case of the dog, we can run or attack. I guess it depends on how big you are and if you are carrying mace!

Let's suppose you attack. Immediately upon sensing a threat, change, or in this case the stress of a mean animal, certain things happen. Sixteen major muscle groups tighten and become ready for action. The red blood cells which carry oxygen to the muscles increase in number. The white blood cells used to fight infection reduce in number. The liver releases glucose or sugar to supply the muscles with their food source in huge amounts. The heart beats faster and stronger. Blood pressure rises. Pupils dilate. The digestive process comes to a near halt. The kidneys reduce their output. The overall metabolism increases by some 50%. You are like a rocket on the launch pad at Cape Kennedy—fueled and ready for blast-off. The latest research from the University of Pittsburg shows that stress hormones are present in our system when under a stressful situation, and these hormones are toxic to brain cells in rats. This might be one explanation why we lose things like our keys when under stress. This was reported by Carla Rohling in the September 3, 1991, issue of Family Circle magazine.

Now let's suppose you decide to run away. Guess what happens? Like an athlete running a race, you will have 16 major muscles immediately tighten, your red blood cell count rises, your white cell count drops, your heart beats faster and stronger, etc. Sound familiar? That's the sympathetic response to stress, and your body does not know if you are going to run away or if you are going to fight. The key point here is that we have only two choices in a stressful situation—to fight or to take flight. The body doesn't know the difference.

Remember the behavior of the caveman? Not that you are like that; but pretend for a moment that you live your life in a state of tension and stress, always fussing and fuming, always complaining and bitter. Your body will do what you tell it to do. If you say to it that you want it to be ready to attack or run, it will prepare itself accordingly. It will stay in that high state of sympathetic response just for you.

As I understand it, we can develop a habit or break a habit in about three weeks. But maybe you have been like this for years. You are ready to blast off any second. In short, your body thinks this is the way it's suppose to be. You would never sit in your car in the driveway and keep revving the engine at very high RPMS, would you? What would happen to your car if you did? It would fall apart. What happens to your body when kept in a sympathetic response state for a long period of time? The heart wears out faster, the blood pressure rises to a pathological state, acid in the muscles increases, leading to bone hitting bone, causing spurs to develop—better known as osteoarthritis. TMJ dysfunction (a condition of abnormality involving the jaw) develops, high sugar concentration occurs, and digestion is affected.

Stress has been reported to be a precipitating factor in many of Modern Man's most common diseases, including heart attack, stroke, diabetes, arthritis, back/neck pain, digestive problems, and many more. By changing our lifestyle and our thinking, we may be able to prevent a tragedy in the future.

Let's suppose you have sustained a neck injury very possibly due to stress. The following diagram explains what happens with an injury and demonstrates the vicious cycle with injuries.

Injury	→	
Muscle Guarding	→	
Stopped Movement	→	
Stiffness	→	← HEADACHES
Decreased Circulation	→	
Increased Weakness	→	← NECK PAIN
Protective Posture	→	
Muscle Spasms	→	← JAW PAIN
More Weakness	→	
Postural Strain	→	← SHOULDER PAIN
Decreased Joint Nutrition	→	
Disc Weakening	→	
More Injuries	→	

I have a friend who gets cold sores on the outside of her mouth whenever she experiences a stressful situation. Remember, one of the effects of the sympathetic response is to lower the white blood cell count, which is used to fight infection. Just maybe her resistance to infection is down, and this is why cold sores occur! One of my employees recently experienced another example of reduced resistance. This person never missed a day of work due to illness in five years. One by one, various events happened to her that gradually wore her down. Her 17-year-old daughter quit school and became involved with drugs; her older daughter with two children moved back home after a divorce and refused to even look for a job or an apartment; her husband did not offer the emotional support needed and actually shunned her. The final straw was when her 16-year-old son ran away and she had no idea of his safety or whereabouts. First she was diagnosed as having a cold, then bronchitis; and finally after three months of being ill, she was diagnosed as having viral pneumonia, was hospitalized, and had to resign because of health reasons. Was it stress that caused the medical problems? Probably not. But one thing is for certain—her physical ability to fight disease was definitely affected.

The most common reason for missed work is the common cold. The second is headaches. I wonder how many people with a cold have a reduced resistance due to stress. For 18 years I have worked with people who suffer from pain. The most common symptoms I treat are neck pain and headaches. I have seen literally hundreds of patients who finally admit to some type of major stress, which they say might be a contributing factor. During, and even after stress, our posture changes significantly.

When we feel good, we stand erect with our shoulders back and head upright. When we feel sad, depressed, or lost, our shoulders slump, our head comes forward, our torso falls forward, and our knees bend. The head on average weighs 12-14 pounds. When it moves forward two inches, it exerts a force of 36 pounds. We are then asking the long, thin muscles up the back of the neck to hold an object weighing three times its normal weight. The muscles can do this for a very short period of time, but eventually, the muscles will become strained and tight. These same muscles attach to the base of the skull and fan out as they connect to it. Passing through the tendinous tissue of attachments lie blood vessels supplying blood to the skull. When the muscles tighten, they squeeze the vessels and prevent blood from reaching the top of the head—not the brain, but the skull which, has more muscle covering.

The tightening of muscles is much the same as crimping a garden hose so all the water won't come out. A reduction of blood creates a vascular headache. This type of headache is very common.

There are many factors which affect our posture. Stress isn't the only one. Unlike a virus, which can be linked directly to illness, or a fall to a fracture, stress is not viewed by some as a direct link or cause to major health problems.

Many physicians treat symptoms and fail to look beyond their scope. I believe that if the medical community would slow down and listen to their patients more (not so much as to what is said, but how it is said), better care would be offered. Often, just mentioning stress to your physician brings about a prescription for some type of drug. Valium seems to be the drug of choice. The problem is not with the doctors, however. Too often we want a quick cure, a magic pill. We can take medication for years, but until we say, "Enough is enough," and change our thinking and our lifestyle, we will continue to treat the symptoms and not the cause.

How about this one? "Oh you have stress. Well, just try to relax. It will be o.k." That's about as ridiculous as telling a hard core addict to "Just say No." Medication certainly has a place in dealing with stress but for only short periods of time. The mind must heal the body.

Stress can lead to clinical depression, and for many people this cycle includes pain. As stress occurs and leads to depression, more pain will develop. Just ask someone who has rheumatoid arthritis. There is a direct relationship between our moods and pain. How do you feel the last day of work before going on a great vacation? Absolutely nothing is going to go wrong. You will feel great all day. No aches or pains. How do you feel several weeks later when you return from your trip? The same old, boring job, the same old problems, etc. You then notice every little ache and pain. As an exercise, complete the Pain/Mood diary below for one week and monitor your reactions.

Mood/Pain Diary

MOOD

	Mon.	Tues.	Wed.	Thurs.	Fri.	Sat.	Sun.
Great							
Awful							

PAIN

	Mon.	Tues.	Wed.	Thurs.	Fri.	Sat.	Sun.
None							
Terrible							

Points to remember

1. Stress is a precipitating factor in many common illnesses.
2. The body reacts the same way whether we fight or take flight.
3. The mind must heal the body.
4. Poor posture is a common cause for headaches. Try to pull your head back in a gliding motion so your ears line up with your shoulders. Practice making a double chin, and this will reduce neck tension.
5. Pain and moods are directly related.

4

Coping Methods

So you had a terrible day! You were late for work, ran out of gas, and then had no money—which you noticed only after filling up the car with gas. During the day, you made several mistakes on the project you were working on, ran over your child's bicycle as you pulled into the driveway, your son was kept after school for discipline problems, and tomorrow you have to meet with his teacher. That dreaded past-due notice came in the mail, dinner was a mess, and your mate hasn't stopped talking about how bad his day was. Stress? Oh yeah! When it rains, it pours, right? That's another way of recognizing when you're under stress—you catch yourself making such a comment.

Getting close to your stress point, huh? If one more thing happens, you'll scream. Let's see what happens. It's now 8:45 p.m., and that precious little son of yours tells you he needs a three-ringed notebook for tomorrow or he will be disciplined again. No, he couldn't have asked you at a more reasonable time. That would be asking too much. What happens? You might yell a little, grind your teeth, knock something over on the way out the door as you slam it, and talk to yourself all the way to the store and back home. Then, when you get back home your mate has the audacity to say, "What the heck is wrong with you, anyway?" This is the first time anyone has asked how your day was. Let the games begin! Gentlemen, start your engines! After several minutes of yelling and arguing, you say the heck with it. You're going to bed. Filled to the brim with the sympathetic responses—how do you sleep?

It takes six hours for a muscle that has been stressed to relax and be quiet. If you went to bed at 10 o'clock, your muscles would finally let go and relax at about 4:00 a.m. You get up at six to start another day with only two hours of muscle rest. How will this day be for you? Sound familiar? After you finally settle down the next evening, where is your energy level? Doesn't it feel good to just lie on the couch and fall asleep? You are healing your body. Last night if you would have performed some type of exercise before going to bed, the six hours required to relax your muscles would have been reduced.

There is a very simple exercise that will take the six hours down to about 30 minutes. It is called Jacobson Relaxation and has been used for years. Another name for this is progressive relaxation exercise. Like many of my patients, you may be one of those who doesn't know what it's like to relax. Or, you may be so geared up that other techniques described later simply won't work for you. By using this technique, you will learn the difference between tension and relaxation.

You can do this either sitting or lying down. To some extent, you can even do this in your car; but the optimum position is in a quiet room or in bed before going to sleep. For years I had difficulty sleeping because of stress and my general inability to relax. In the course of a year, I might have slept all the way through five or six nights. After learning and doing these exercises, I now have no problem. Remember the 16 major muscle groups which tighten and all the sugar present in our system when under stress? Well, the effect of this exercise routine is to burn off the sugar and adrenaline, thereby relaxing the muscles.

Soft music may be helpful to you. Get into a comfortable position. Loosen all tight clothing. Start by closing your eyes and feel yourself breathing. Feel the air going in and out. Place your hand on your stomach and make your hand rise and fall as you breathe in and out. Breathe slowly and deeply, holding your breath at the top of your inspiration, and then slowly exhale. Another major principle of good posture, which also applies to the reduction of stress, is the breathing pattern. An excellent rule to follow that will help prevent headaches and help facial muscles to relax is to place the tip of your tongue on the roof of your mouth, keeping your teeth apart, with your lips together. Breathe deeply and slowly. This is imperative.

Begin by squeezing your dominant hand as hard as you can and holding it tightly closed for five seconds. Think about how this feels. Think of the tension and how uncomfortable it is. Now relax your grip and open your hand. Think about how this feels, and see if you notice any warmth. Tighten the forearm and hand of your dominant side and hold it for five seconds, squeezing as hard as you can. Feel the uncomfortable sensation. Let go. Let your arm and hand fall for five seconds. How is your breathing? Is it slow and deep? Next squeeze your hand, forearm, and shoulder absolutely as hard as you can. Harder and harder! Let go and allow the entire arm and hand to fall and relax. Rest your dominant side and repeat the procedure on the other side, part by part. After doing the recessive side, move to the legs and start with the dominant leg.

Bring your toes up toward the ceiling, keeping your heel in contact with a surface such as the bed or floor. Tighten again as hard as you can, holding for five seconds. Let your leg go limp and relax for five seconds. How is your breathing? Is it slow and deep? Tighten your leg at the knee, then relax. Move to the thigh. Tighten and relax. Repeat this procedure on the other leg.

Get the picture? You can do this on any muscle you want. If your eyes become tired and sore from driving, typing, reading, etc., squeeze your eyes closed as tight as possible, hold for five seconds, then relax. Repeat this until your eyes feel better. Be sure to do one eye at a time if you're driving! I learned years ago never to assume—and be specific at all times!

Breathing

As you work more on your stress management, you will learn terms like Yoga, biofeedback, meditation, mental imagery, and autogenics. Common to each of these is proper breathing. It is essential to any stress reduction program. It's easy to do and obviously can be done anywhere. If you are ever in a social situation where your behavior must be controlled, deep breathing will get you through the event. Watch elite athletes, such as Olympians, just prior to their event. You will see them breathing very deeply and concentrating. Sprinters will stand behind their starting blocks and breathe deeply. It creates a calming effect on muscles. It will eliminate the body's automatic reaction of shallow breathing when a stressful event occurs. Deep breathing "turns on" your relaxation response.

Place a hand on your stomach and inhale. You should feel your stomach rise. As you exhale, your stomach should drop. Sit up as straight as possible and roll your shoulders back. This will allow greater space for your lungs to expand. Watch professional singers. They always stand and sit up straight for better breathing. As an exercise, sit in a chair and lean forward. Take a deep breath and see how long you can hold it. Now sit up as straight as possible, roll your shoulders back, and stick your chest out. Now take a deep breath. Did you notice how much more air you could get by sitting up straight? An exercise to teach yourself proper breathing techniques is to lie flat on the bed and place an empty glass or cup on your stomach. If you inhale properly, the glass will rise. Practice this once a day for about two minutes, and in just a couple of days you will have the technique mastered.

Remember the rule: lips together, teeth apart, and tongue on the roof of your mouth. As you inhale, do so through your nose. The air will be cleaned and warmed. Breathe in as long as possible, then hold your breath at the end of your inspiration for a few seconds. When you exhale, imagine you have wrapped your lips around a straw and you want all the air to be blown out through the straw. Push all the air out and then some! We have dead air spaces in the bottom of our lungs and you can get this dead air out by allowing fresh air in. If you are alone at home or in your office, you can take it one step further. Put a pillow, book, or both hands on your stomach. As you exhale, lean forward, pulling the pillow, book, etc. into your stomach. This technique will assist in getting all the air out. Should you become a little dizzy, just stop a few moments and relax. It will pass. This procedure can be repeated for as long as you choose. But usually only a few deep breaths will suffice to calm you down. This technique is given to patients with chronic lung problems and helps them breathe much better.

Again, I must emphasize that proper breathing is one of the most important aspects of any stress management program.

Mental imagery

Want to take a vacation at the beach, but you can't afford it? Wish you could visit the mountains, but you have no vacation time left? Are you feeling that if you could just get away, everything would be fine? Well, you can take that trip, escape for a while, and feel rejuvenated—all without leaving your living room or office. It's called mental imagery. Your body will follow your mind. If you tell it healthy, positive things, it will respond in a certain way. If you tell it negative, stressful things, it will respond in another way. You can take that trip or escape for a while in your mind. The body won't know it did not actually experience the event.

Begin by finding a quiet place. Loosen all tight clothing and sit or lie in a comfortable position. Close your eyes and focus your attention on your breathing. Think about how deep and slow it is. Each of us has a place in our past where life was great, a place where we felt alive and comfortable. It might have been in the woods, on a mountain, or at the ocean, etc. Or you may have a place you have always wanted to visit and can only imagine how beautiful it must be. Imagine that place now. For the sake of this exercise, let's pretend it's a forest.

It's a Fall day, and you are deep in the forest all alone. There isn't another human for miles. The afternoon sun is shining through the tall tree tops, and shadows are seen waving across the path below you as you lean back against a grassy embankment. Never before have you seen such brilliant colors. The large, crisp leaves scrape one another and occasionally crinkle against the bark as the wind floats them to the ground. The smell of pine pierces your nose and for a moment reminds you of a fireplace. You feel warm inside. Squirrels bound and leap on the ground and from tree to tree. The smell of a rotted stump is pushed past your nostrils, and, the musty odor takes you aback for a moment. The birds sing just for you, and off in the distance you hear the rapping of a woodpecker. Your arms and legs feel so heavy that you lean back and sink into the bank and fall effortlessly asleep. Everything is right with the world.

You can do this type of exercise as often as you choose and for as long as you like. Should you be a Type A personality, like myself, it will probably take a few times to practice this before you are proficient and comfortable. At first, you might have difficulty reaching your spot because of outside noises and other distractions. Don't let those bother you, and don't dwell on them. If you pay attention to the distractions, you will be giving them importance. And they are not important. Not at all! If you would practice this for a period of three weeks, a habit would be formed, and mental imagery would then feel natural.

After I mentally escape for a short time, I often write my feelings down so I can read them at a later date and hopefully enjoy the same experience of that particular place. One Saturday I was on the "pitypot," feeling sorry for myself after a long, arduous week at work. Rather than ruining my weekend, I escaped and afterward felt fantastic. I felt energized and wrote a poem which I will share with you here.

AROUND ME

With my body full of wear and my mind feeling drained
While helping fellow-man, my life it felt strained.
I viewed this week's decisions and wondered if they were right.
Sometimes the stress of life takes away my fight.

I asked God if it's worth it. Is this what's meant to be?
I asked Him to help me, to guide me and to see.
I watched the morn awaken and the sun come through the trees.
I slowly felt relaxed. My soul felt at ease.

Shades of green began to wave as the wind stirred around.
Nature was in my ear. I felt every sound.
Squirrels began to leap, appearing not to care.
I watched them intensely as if I were there.

I smelled the flowers in their bed. Petals yawned with grace.
They put their spell upon me. Each with its own face.
A fallen leaf moved about as if not of the scheme.
I had learned Nature's way. Knew it fit the theme.

I was like the lonely leaf, not taking care of me.
Dwelling on my woes. Not taking time to see.
I anticipate tomorrow. Life is now in line.
Relaxed and rested, I'm ready for the climb.

Exercise

So you say you're not a Type A personality, but a "flaming A" personality, and sitting still for ten minutes is just about impossible. Your idea of relaxation certainly does not include mental imagery, because you'd go stir-crazy! Well, that was me sometime ago, and I can certainly relate to that. Simply because I overcame my inability to sit still and relax, doesn't mean you can do that. That's what reformed smokers say. Don't they?

Rejoice! For all of you who must always be doing something, there is a stress management technique for you as well. It's called exercise. And you will love it. Remember the Jacobson Technique which was explained earlier. I know that deep breathing and contracting your muscles for 15 minutes is not what you could tolerate. These exercises are for the buffs who go out and run all weekend, play racquetball by the hour and drink carrot juice. Oh, that's not you, either? I assure you that if you can walk, you will benefit from this section.

Reviewing for a moment, picture the body tense with sixteen major muscle groups tightened, the system full of adrenaline, heart racing, sugar pumping throughout, and blood pressure elevated.

Guess what exercise does for the body? It lowers sugar level, makes the heart more efficient, creates relaxed muscles, and is an aid in lowering blood pressure. It also helps with exchange of blood gasses, strengthens bones, and creates a sense of general well-being. The optimum level of exercise is to obtain an aerobic level three times per week for 30 minutes each time. Two general and safe rules to follow are: First, while exercising you should be able to carry on a conversation. This means you are functioning at a safe level and not overdoing things. Next, if you know how to find your pulse, count the beats for a period of 30 seconds and multiply it by two. That will tell you how many times your heart is beating per minute. Subtract your age from 220 and then multiply that number by 80%. That is known as your target rate. While exercising, your heart rate should not exceed your target rate. If it does, simply rest until the rate drops. Naturally, if symptoms persist, consult medical help. The best time to take your pulse is immediately after exercising. Don't wait even five minutes.

There are many types of exercises you can do. The bottom line is to pick an activity that is enjoyable and fun for you. Doing calisthenic type exercises by themselves can be quite boring and mundane. I have prescribed these for 18 years and very seldom found a patient who loved them. Two of the best all-around exercises are walking and swimming. Every part of your body can be worked, and you will rid yourself of stress symptoms. But again, make it enjoyable. An example of what not to do is riding in a golf cart and throwing your club because you didn't get the shot you wanted. This, too, I have learned from experience.

To prevent injury, always follow this rule: Heat-stretch-strengthen. We should warm a muscle with a hot shower or wet heat and then slowly stretch the muscle for about ten to fifteen minutes before we strengthen it through our activity. When stretching a muscle, never bounce, but hold for the count of five and then relax. Do about ten repetitions. When you feel tight or stressed, a good routine is to do some general stretching exercises. These can be done at work or at home.

Exercises to reduce stress

1. Head Circles   Look left, roll your chin across your chest to your right. Look right and repeat.
2. Shoulder Shrugs   Shrug your shoulders, then slowly relax.
3. Ceiling Reach   Stretch your arm straight above your head and reach for the ceiling.

4. Back Scratch	Reach over your shoulder and scratch the middle of your back, reach from underneath and scratch again. (Repeat with other arm.)
5. Knee to Chest	Raise your knee to your chest, with both arms pull it higher. (Repeat, using other leg.)
6. Knee Straighten	Straighten each knee, keeping thigh flat on the chair. (Repeat, using other leg.)
7. Ankle Alphabet	Draw the letters of the alphabet in the air with your feet.
8. Prayer	Hands together in the praying position, raise elbows up toward ceiling.
9. Chair Check	Bend forward over your legs and look under your chair.
10. Hug	Wrap both arms around your shoulders—give yourself a hug.

If your legs can move, you can overcome the symptoms of stress by walking. If you have difficulty sleeping at night, go for a walk before going to bed (provided of course that you live in a safe neighborhood). A ten minute walk will do more for your rest than sleeping drugs. It will create a natural state of relaxation. Remember the Six Hour Rule for muscles to relax? This, too, will help calm those tightened areas. You don't need to have a model's body and purple tights along with skinny legs to exercise! Almost any kind of exercise will be beneficial.

Did you ever get upset with someone and say, "Just leave me alone!"? And then you cleaned the house from top to bottom—scrubbing floors, washing windows, mopping, cleaning cupboards, etc. How did you feel after two hours of this vigorous activity? Didn't you say to yourself, "Now I know I was supposed to be mad about something, but I don't remember what it was!"? How did you feel the last time you washed and waxed the car or worked outside in the yard all day? Pretty good, didn't you? You were doing a form of stress management exercises.

I have a nail board out in my work shed, and after a really bad day I will sometimes go out and pound nails until I'm exhausted. This works great for ridding myself of stress before going into the house and possibly demonstrating displacement by taking out my frustrations on those around me. One time after pounding nails and feeling so good, I attempted to lift the board and discovered that I had done too good a job— I nailed the board into my new workbench and had to get a crowbar to pry it loose. Sometimes exercise can be too vigorous.

Regardless of the type of exercise you choose, make sure it's enjoyable, or your good intentions will quickly be laid to rest. Exercise produces a chemical called endorphine, which has a calming effect on the body. This is responsible for the way we feel after an orgasm or after a satisfying meal. Endorphine also is responsible for the runner's high. So if you want to be active and feel good emotionally and physically, exercise three times a week for thirty minutes.

Attitude

There are two basic principles in controlling your stress. Without control over both of these, your program will be difficult at best. The first is easy. It's controlling your breathing. The second is more difficult. That is to change your attitude. Without a re-focus on what is really important in life and a change to the behavior of being good to yourself, things may be very tough for you.

Did you ever stop to realize that you feel a certain way because you want to? You can control your thoughts. Your thoughts control your feelings. Therefore, you—not your spouse, boss, or neighbors—control how you feel. What you feel is by choice. If you feel under pressure and stressed out, it's your own fault!

Remembering that the body reacts to what the mind tells it, I'd like you to experience this exercise. You will need someone to read it to you. It should be read slowly and meticulously.

Start by closing your eyes. Imagine you have a lemon in the palm of your hand. Roll it around and gently squeeze it. Feel every part of its texture. Think about the color as well as the shape. Now imagine you are cutting the lemon with a very sharp knife. Let the juices drip and then run onto your hand. Think about how it smells. Now put the lemon onto your tongue. Suck in some juice.

O.K., the test is over. Did you pucker? Can you still sense the sourness? Was there really a lemon? No. It was all in your mind, and your body reacted to what you thought.

Think about this. What we believe is what we see. Because our physical senses appear to relay information from the outside world to our brain, we may believe our state of mind is controlled entirely by the feedback we receive. This belief contributes to a sense of ourselves as separate entities who are largely isolated and feel alone in an uncaring, fragmented world. This can leave us with the impression that the world we see is the cause and we are the effect.

Let's consider the possibility that this type of thinking is upsidedown and backward. What would happen if we believed that what we see is determined by the thoughts in our minds? Perhaps we could entertain an idea that for the moment seems unnatural and foreign to us; namely, that our thoughts are the cause and what we see is the effect. It would then make no sense to blame the world or those in it for the misery and pain we experience, because it will be possible to consider perception as a "mirror, not a fact." We react by what we perceive as truth, not what is fact.

Consider once again that the mind may be like a motion picture camera, projecting our internal state onto the world. When our mind is peaceful, the world and the people in it appear to us as peaceful. We can choose to wake up in the morning and see a friendly world through glasses that filter out everything except love. Each of us has the power to direct our minds to replace the feelings of being upset, depressed, and fearful with the feeling of inner peace.

I am tempted to believe that I am upset because of what others do or because of circumstances and events which seem beyond my control. I may experience being upset as some form of anger, jealousy, resentment, or depression. Actually, all these feelings represent some form of fear that I am experiencing. When I recognize I have the choice between being fearful or experiencing love by extending love to others, I no longer need to be upset for any reason. Throughout the day, whenever I am tempted to be fearful, I remind myself that I can experience love instead.

Let's pretend you work with a very mean, hardened supervisor. No matter what you do, it's never good enough. He never gives any praise and, on the contrary, often ridicules you and others. Picture this person as the meanest person on the face of the earth. You hate your job, but you are stuck in this position. Now, can you remember what you felt the last time you had a vacation? How did you feel the morning of your last day at work? If you're like most of us, you probably felt as though no matter what happened that day, things were going to go well. And indeed, they did. Do you think your boss was any different that particular day? No. Remember—he's always mean and hateful. It was your perception of him that changed.

How do you respond to your children? Can a child one time do something wrong in your eyes and receive a reprimand, while he may do the exact same thing another time and you don't scold him because things are going just great? Think about the mixed messages you are sending him. And of course the opposite is also true. Things are only as awful as we perceive them to be!

One thing eighteen years as a physical therapist has taught me is that for a person to become better, he must want it. Is there anything you ever wanted in life, *really* wanted, that you did not achieve? If a person is a whiny, wimpy person who is very dependent on others, he will respond much slower to treatment. His body will repair itself more slowly, and results will not be as good as the person who believes he will get back to normal. Unfortunately, I have seen the negative aspect of this over and over with patients covered under worker's compensation and when there is a lawsuit involved.

In 1968, Chase Kimbell at the University of Rochester Medical School divided into four groups patients who were going to receive a heart procedure; their attitudes toward surgery determined the groups they were put in.

Group #1: These individuals were well adjusted. They coped well under stress and were able to continue with life even though they were sick. They tended to be individuals who were realistic, had good insight, and possessed a keen sense of awareness. They believed surgery was a positive experience. There were

13 individuals in this category. One died due to equipment malfunction, nine became better, and three stayed the same.

Group #2: These were secondary-gain type people who looked at open heart surgery as a process that would keep them from getting worse. In short, they believed the procedure was designed to keep them about the same. They did not want to improve, nor did they want to get worse. There were 15 patients in this category. One died, one became better, and thirteen stayed the same.

Group #3: These were called "deniers." They denied anxiety and felt uneasy but would not talk about it. They were sleepless, distant, and withdrawn and could not talk about the upcoming procedure. There were twelve patients in this category. Four died, three became better, three stayed the same, and three became worse.

Group #4: These were depressed individuals. They viewed life as a struggle. They did not care what happened. They viewed surgery as something the physician wanted. The underlying theme was that the procedure would not help. There were fifteen patients in this category. Eleven died, and four became worse.

Yes, attitude is the key to your success or failure. The choice is yours. Do fewer things and do them better! Support groups such a AA have great slogans, like "Easy Does It" and "One Day At a Time." I use two in particular that I learned somewhere along the way. I ask myself—"Does it really matter?" and "Does anyone in Chicago know about this?" One day I was feeling pretty good about myself, because I had on a new outfit. That was until I drove over the curb at the convenience store and spilled coffee all over myself. My first reaction was to do some finger aerobics like "shooting a bird," or whatever. I then asked myself, "Does anyone in Chicago know I spilled coffee on my new pants?" That calmed me down immediately, and I went about my day as if nothing had happened. My staff, of course, kidded me about needing a catheter.

There was one time when my little saying about Chicago did not help. I flew back to Orlando from Chicago, and my luggage was lost. As I was in the middle of having a panic attack and throwing a temper tantrum, my wife tried to calm me down by saying, "Does anyone in Chicago know about this?" I won't print what I said about the person in Chicago who lost my luggage!

Meditation helps me change my poor attitude. You can buy any of several books on the topic or discuss it with someone in your community. Basically, what I do is turn off all the lights, play soft music, and sit in the Yoga position. I start by breathing from deep in my stomach three times. I touch my thumbs and index fingers together and begin to relax. I then focus my attention on seven different areas progressively. These are: the base of the spine, groin, stomach, heart, throat, and forehead. I take three deep breaths at each area, thinking of love and peace. The last area is the top of my head, where I imagine an egg filled with a glowing light of peace and kindness. I picture it breaking and covering my entire body. The process takes anywhere from fifteen to thirty minutes. When I finish, I feel as though I had been relaxed for hours. The best time of day to meditate is as soon as you wake up or just before going to sleep. That is when we are most receptive.

The paradox of life is not the outward things, but the answer to peace and serenity is within us at all times. All we need to do is let it out. I wrote a poem about my experiences meditating which I will share with you now.

THE GIFT

Close your eyes, oh little one, and let the spirit flow.
He'll guide you and protect you and show you where to go.

When I relax and search for peace, the spirit lets me see.
He's deep inside all of us. In you and also me.

To be content and happy as I journey through the maze,
My spirit leads and guides me. He takes away my haze.

Let go! Let go! And stop the strain. Life can be such fun.
When I center on myself, my spirit and I are one.

Points to remember
1. Do deep breathing exercises from deep in youe stomach.
2. Do one positive thing for someone each day.
3. Give in periodically.
4. Accept what you cannot change.
5. Ask yourself, "Do they know about this in Chicago?"
6. Engage in physical activity or relaxation exercises at the end of each day.
7. Remember that you are responsible for your own feelings.
8. Take a mental vacation. Picture a place you want to be and enjoy it for a while.
9. Do fewer things, and do them better.
10. If you think that if one more thing happens, you'll scream, or if you say, "That's the straw that broke the camel's back," then you are feeling the effects of stress.
11. Jacobson Relaxation technique can relax your muscles in about 30 minutes as opposed the to six hours it takes without this method.
12. Good posture includes the rule: Lips together, teeth apart, tongue on roof of your mouth.
13. Exercise at least three times each week for 30 minutes each time.

5
Worry and Guilt

Our nervous system cannot tell the difference between an imagined experience and a real experience. It simply reacts to what we think or imagine to be true. We act and respond not according to how things really are but according to the image our minds hold of how things are. With positive thinking, we vividly imagine in our minds how things are or will be. Unfortunately, the opposite is also true. If we picture ourselves as a failure, we most certainly will fail. It is what we want played out in our imagination.

Earlier you learned that there are two choices to stress which are to fight or take flight from a problem or stressor. There is one other choice we have, but it's counterproductive. It is called worrying! At least when we fight or take flight, we are doing something. We are taking some type of action. When we worry, we do nothing except waste time and energy and create more stress on ourselves. Worrying is like banging your head against the wall. Nothing is accomplished.

Because you may have failed in the past with, let's say, a relationship, you might be worried that you will fail in the present with another relationship. A person has to start in the present to acquire some maturity so the future may be better than the past. The present and future depend on learning new habits and new ways of looking at old problems. There simply isn't any future in digging continually into the past. Always criticizing yourself for past mistakes and errors does not help matters but, rather, tends to perpetuate the very behavior you would like to change. Memories of past failures can adversely affect present performance. If you dwell on those failures, the conclusion usually reached is, I failed yesterday, so I will fail today. The minute we change our minds and stop giving power to the past, the past and all its mistakes lose power over us.

Worry is defined as being immobilized in the present by ideas that are not going to happen in the future. Worry makes us less effective and wastes time. When we worry, we keep dwelling on the end result, picturing it to ourselves as a possibility and assuming it will probably happen. This constant repetition makes the end result seem more and more real. After a time, the systems in our bodies generate the appropriate reactions—fear, anxiety, discouragement. All these are appropriate to the end result you are worrying about.

Some of us confuse worry with caring. These are not synonymous. The mother who always seems to be worrying about her children can be looked upon by others as a caring mother. They might say something like, "Oh, isn't she a good parent? She's always worrying about her children." Nothing could be farther than the truth. In addition to being labeled as a caring person, there are other payoffs of worrying. One is that we don't have to take risks, and another is that it justifies self-defeating behavior. It also helps us to avoid changing; and, most sadly of all, it keeps us from living!

To eliminate worry, once again use your mind—your attitude. It's the job of the conscious mind to decide what you want, to select the goals you are after. Concentrate on what you want, rather than on what you *don't* want. To spend time and energy on things you don't want by worrying is not rational. When President Dwight Eisenhower was General Eisenhower in World War II, he was asked, "What would have been the effect upon the Allied cause if the troops had been thrown back into the sea from the beaches of Italy?" Eisenhower replied, "It would have been very bad, but I never allow my mind to work that way." We must learn to do our work, act upon the best assumptions available, and let the results take care of themselves.

Guilt is another very negative emotion which can prevent us from living and enjoying life. It can haunt us our entire life.

If you have harmed someone in your past which makes you feel guilty, make amends today—even if they are now dead! Write a letter, or picture in your mind the act of forgiveness. Don't carry the burden around another minute. It is excess baggage and does you no good whatsoever. We don't need to directly communicate with someone in order to forgive them. You can do it in your mind.

Points to remember
1. Admit when you make a mistake.
2. Be kind to yourself and others.
3. Remember that what you give to others you give to yourself.
4. Try not to cry over spilled milk. Think of your past defeats as sandpaper which brings out the grain of life.
5. Get off the "pitypot."
6. Don't be a martyr.
7. Don't accept a substitute for forgiving others.
8. Live for today.
9. Accept responsibility for your actions.
10. The only importance of the past is to learn from it.

PART TWO

Daily Stressors

6
Self-Esteem/Activities/ Laughter

I believe the basis for successful stress management is our self-esteem and our attitude. When either one or both of these are negative, our stress reaction elevates. When you feel good about yourself, nothing can harm you. "Sticks and stones will break my bones, but words will never hurt me." There is a great deal of truth to this childhood rhyme. Changing or improving your self-esteem and attitude is a lifelong process. And it can be done. It's really fun! If you experience major life changes in excess, in a short time you can suffer mentally. That is what you learned in Part One. If you allow daily stress to get to you in little pieces, that too can harm you. Daily stressors such as trying to make ends meet, long lines, lack of sleep, no time for recreation, being late for appointments, burned cooking, and even broken shoelaces can seem to drive some people bonkers and off the deep end at times.

Daily stressors that you think (there are those words again— "I think") are annoying create health problems. Always thank only yourself for the pleasant state of affairs you are having. If permitted, daily stress can lead to depression, lack of physical energy, anger, stomach pain, frustration, insomnia, and low motivation.

How do you feel after a long, hard day at work when everything goes wrong? Couple this with an argument with your family members that night, and maybe even throw in a second bad day at work. Now how do you feel? Want to cook a large meal or have the neighbors over for coffee? Do you really want to attend that P.T.A. meeting? Any trouble sleeping? And how is your stomach? Do I hear rumblings in the gut? Congratulations! You are a regular part of the daily rat race. But you don't have to be. What you feel is by choice. The answer is inside you. Relax and shut down the chatter. Listen deep inside, and let all the love and peace out that you want. The keys are self-esteem and attitude.

Do you ever get frustrated because you play the game correctly and do what you know to be right? You studied hard, always paid your taxes, married, and bought a house. But why aren't you happy? Why aren't you ahead? Maybe we put too much emphasis on material things, which we equate with success, and not enough on inner peace and enjoyment. Did you ever say or think that money buys happiness? Did you ever say, "Yeah, but I'd sure like to find out if money buys happiness for just one day." I have treated hundreds of multi-millionaires, and I can assure you that money does not buy happiness. I have seen alcohol abuse, drug abuse, and depression in many of these families. Human emotions cross all socioeconomic lines. Human emotions know no color, race, or financial status. I think we spend too much time chasing some dream or rainbow we think will make us happy, while all the time it is inside us. Unlike the fairy tales, life is not always happily ever after. We all have bad days or panic attacks. How each of us responds is what is important.

Did you ever have a math problem that no matter how hard you tried the answer wouldn't come? So you walked away only to return later. And what happened? You solved it immediately. Did you ever try so hard to get a great golf shot that you topped it? How about the times you just couldn't hit that softball or get a strike in bowling? What happened when you finally relaxed and just let go? A great golf shot, a base hit, or a strike on the alley. As a kid, did you ever try to walk a balance beam or walk down the railroad tracks? Whenever I tried it, I always fell off if I tried too hard. It was when I relaxed that I could go on forever and have no problem. Maybe life is like that.

When our self-esteem is low, certain things naturally occur. We make poor decisions. Think of the person who is mad and says, "I'll show him. I quit my job," only to realize the next day what has happened. We lose patience easily and don't care to solve daily problems. After a rotten day, all we want to do is vegetate on the couch or go to bed early. When we have panic attacks or beat up ourselves emotionally, that is the time to be alone, rest, and recuperate our body and our mind. Successful stress management is a selfish program. If you are a fixer, a martyr, or think you are superhuman, controlling your stress will be difficult but fun to achieve.

A lady in one of my classes once shared with the group how she pulls in to heal and say "no." When things are bad and she doesn't want to be bothered by her family, she wears a red apron. When the family members see the red apron, they know to stay clear. A gentleman once told me he wears a special baseball cap to warn everyone to leave him alone. Don't volunteer when you are down. It is perfectly all right to sleep and allow your mind and body to repair themselves.

When your self-esteem rises, life is peaceful. That is when you should make decisions or commitments. That is the time to be intimate. Sharing your feelings is one of the best stress reducers there is. As a test, put yourself in a controversy. Start your statements with the phrases "I feel" or "I think." Listen to these two statements and notice how one is soft and the other is hard: "You can do better with your homework" or "I feel you can do better with your homework." When you say something in a factual manner, then I have the right to react if I choose. When you say something through your feelings, I should not react in a negative manner. One way to build self-esteem is to have others listen to you. When people listen to us, we feel important and that what we say matters. The best way for people to listen is to start out a statement with "I feel." It's not what you say but how you say it. Get close, speak calmly, make eye contact, and show open-minded body language.

Another great way to build self-esteem is through activities. These can be a fantastic diversion to daily stressors and gradually increase your self-esteem. Is there something you wanted to do but felt there was no way you'd ever accomplish it? Or is there something you really want to do but feel totally inadequate? I'm here to tell you that whatever you want to do you can. If you should happen not to be a success—so what! Life is fun! Your activity also should be fun. Try to find one new activity each year. It will expand your horizons and help get you off the pitypot.

A mechanic I'm not. I've never had a minute's worth of training, and don't know one tool from another. When I have a flat tire, I ask the neighbor lady to fix it for me. For years I bought gas at the full service pump, because I didn't know where the tank was. Get the picture? Give me any mechanical action that requires the use of my hands, and I fall apart. My friends call me "ten thumbs"! Three years ago, I took a class through adult education at the high school on stained glass. What the heck! I felt creative. And to my surprise and delight, I did just fine at it. To this day I can feel my ego elevate when I step back and admire a lamp, a sun catcher, or a framed piece that I did all alone! My friends praise me. I could even sell some of these items if I wanted to. But I give them all away. You see, I'm doing this for me and for the pure and simple pleasure of it.

The last time (come to think of it, the only time) I ever had music lessons was in the third grade at Audubon Elementary School in 1957. I love 50s/60s music, and I enjoy the saxophone. One day a friend overheard me saying something to the effect that I wanted to play the sax some day. As a Christmas gift, she purchased a month's rental and lessons. Remember now, I don't know one note from another. And the last musical instrument I played at Audubon was the violin. Frustrated, I smashed it on the dresser into a million pieces, never to touch another instrument until this year at age 42! Here I am into my sixth lesson, and I'm already playing simple songs. But more importantly, I'm having a great time learning a new activity, and I'm proud as can be of my accomplishments. It doesn't matter how good I will become, because it's all for fun. Life should be that way!

Other activities I've taken up include roller-blading, gardening, writing poetry, and snow skiing. Some of these are costly, and others take only time. Find an activity, and have fun. That's the important thing. Have fun! And, by the way, these should be done alone for the most part. Take a magazine to work and read about your hobby during lunch. It's a great way to escape.

Beating the daily blues and having a good time in life should be a goal for each of us. If you're not getting one good belly laugh a day, something is wrong. Had a bad day at work? Rent a comedy and laugh until you cry. Laughter clears the sinuses, improves respiration, lowers pulse rate, lowers blood pressure, and reduces pain. Patients who come to my clinic are always commenting about how much we laugh and how nice it is to visit a medical place such as this. Some patients don't want to be discharged because of the fun we have getting them better!

I personally believe Bill Cosby is the most amusing comedian I have ever heard. Several other people must think so as well because of his reported wealth. He makes us laugh at ourselves and at things that have happened to each of us. He makes life fun and funny!

It's also important to be spontaneous. Don't be rigid in your thinking. It will make you old before your time. Look at problems as challenges. Order a different food on the menu next time you eat out. Wear a tie that doesn't match, take a different route to work, put your left leg in your pants first instead of the right leg, or take a picnic lunch to work and spread out on the grounds. Be creative. Be special, because you are! Be spontaneous!

Do you feel bored, blah, or just plain drained? You already have learned who is to blame. Why is it that Monday through Thursday we feel drained and run down after work? No energy and that tired feeling best describes our moods after work. The more things go wrong at work, the worse we feel. But lo and behold, on Friday we come to life. We are ready to go out to dinner, take in a movie, go to the mall, play miniature golf, etc. Where did we get all that energy? Our bodies don't know what day it is. Again, it's our minds telling us to be tired, bored, and boring! After work, try anything that's different from the norm. Take the kids to a park, go for a drive, or play music you don't normally listen to. Go fishing right from work, take a different way home, or even refuse to cook. Better yet, make the meal a group effort in which everyone helps. Again, the point is to try something different and to have fun doing it.

Points to remember
1. Positive self-esteem and attitude are crucial to managing stress.
2. What we feel is by choice.
3. When esteem is low, physically rest. Don't volunteer; learn to say no; and get some sleep, allowing the body and mind to heal.
4. Share your feelings. They aren't right or wrong; they just are.
5. Activities are great for building self-esteem. Find a new one every year.
6. If you're not getting one good laugh a day, something is wrong.

7
Purging/Friendships/ Nutrition

Purging

Did you ever throw something, swear, or finally tell somebody off in no uncertain terms? While I'm not advocating such behavior, these are examples of purging. It's a case of the classic pressure cooker where we just couldn't take it any more and we let it fly. The problem with this type of behavior is that we usually need to repair a bridge the next day. We apologize and say it will never happen again. At least until the next time. And so on. Exploding like this is better than imploding and taking it all internally until we develop health problems.

There are two general ways to accomplish purging. One is verbal, and the other is physical. Some examples of verbal purging are "controlled complaining," singing, yelling, and—for me—playing my sax! We already discussed most methods of physical purging, such as exercising. Remember my nail board? One method not covered thus far is writing.

One way to get it out is to keep an actual journal. By writing down your thoughts and feelings, you will release tension. Be as specific as possible regarding the stressors. What upset you, why, when, and how did you feel? You may just find a pattern in addition to helping rid your body of stress.

"Controlled complaining" is to find a partner whom you trust thoroughly. With this person, you know all your thoughts and actions will remain confidential. Whatever you say won't be repeated—ever! When you are having a panic attack, which we all experience, or just a bad day in general, go to your partner—or call him on the phone. Feel free to say anything you want in any way you want for a set period of time. Your partner says nothing. Absolutely no advice is given. That's the last thing you need at this time. You see, that's another problem. Too many people are willing to give advice on things they know nothing about. After the time is up, your partner says to stop and you thank him for the assistance and hang up or leave his work area. The matter is never again discussed! This method is a fantastic way to get rid of steam. It must be pointed, quick, and finished. Don't dwell on it.

Don't you find it very frustrating to visit a co-worker on a Saturday night, expecting to have an enjoyable time of cards or games, and you find the conversation always seems to go back to work in a negative way? Maybe you had a problem with Bill at work last Monday, and it was settled in your mind by Tuesday. Now your friend and co-worker had a problem with Bill yesterday. Your friend harps on a subject you have already dealt with, and one of two things will happen. You will get all wound up again about, Bill or you will become upset with your friend. The next time you are in this situation, lay a simple ground rule. There should be no talk about work during your time of play. The spouses will appreciate this as well. Purge in a controlled manner.

This also applies to home life. Set aside the first ten minutes every night, if needed, for the family to get it all out, and then do not allow another negative comment. Have your children watch and participate. What better way for them to learn a healthy method of communication? If any family member makes a negative comment the rest of the night, have them pay a fine into a kitty. When there is enough money, give it to a non-profit organization. Don't spend it on a fun activity. Remember, it's a penalty.

And what about singing (or in my case, croaking)? How do you feel after a long, hot shower when you've been singing up a storm? Singing is also a form of physical exercise that is good for the body and soul. The louder the better. Many times I will go for a drive and play my favorite tapes while singing at the top of my lungs—with the windows closed, of course.

Writing is a great catharsis for pent-up frustrations. It can be used on anyone. Only you will know what is written, so charge away. Have a splendid time. Mad at the boss, a friend, your spouse, or the ever-famous mother-in-law? Write them a letter. Be certain you won't be disturbed, have plenty of pencils and lots of paper. Now is the time to get it all out. Write absolutely anything. There's one important rule to follow. Don't mail it, and don't leave it out in the open where someone will find it, or there will be problems.

The last muscles to relax and let go when you fall asleep are those around the face and side of your head. These seem to be a collecting pot for tension and stress. That is, they show the greatest sign of wear and tear. You have probably heard about worry lines on the face. Place your fingertips above your ears and bite down. Now place your fingertips on the side of your face and bite down. Did you feel these muscles tighten? When you tense or tighten these muscles while awake, it's called clenching. When you tighten these while asleep and grind your teeth, it's called bruxing.

People who have difficulty sleeping, waking up with headaches or a stiff neck, or experience jaw pain may possibly have TMJ Dysfunction. If not treated, a multitude of serious symptoms can develop. Stress is related to this diagnosis, and something as simple as writing your thoughts in letter form to someone who upsets you or writing a list of aggravations may be helpful in controlling some stress. It should prove beneficial for a good night's sleep. As with anything new, try it for three weeks before you judge the results.

There are two simple things you can do in order to rest better. Use a feather pillow (preferably down filled), not a foam pillow. Foam pillows will push your head forward, causing your front teeth to touch. When the teeth touch, the muscles you felt earlier on the side of your face tighten. This is an automatic response. Try it now. Separate your teeth only enough to slide a piece of paper between them. Now tip your head forward. Did you feel your teeth touch? Foam pillows will push the head forward, causing facial muscle tension during sleep. Did you ever wake up with a headache in the morning after using a hard pillow in a motel? Now you know the cause. The second approach to a good night's rest is to ask your dentist about a mouthpiece like football players wear or a device called an anterior deprogrammer. I use the deprogrammer on bad nights after a stressful day. It's made of a smooth material like a bowling ball and fits over my top two front teeth. My jaws and teeth never lock down because the teeth slide around on the smooth surface. I never wake with a headache or any facial pain.

I have long held the belief that the most difficult role in America is to be a single working mom. The second most difficult is to be a married working mom. Mothers who work often begin the day at 6 A.M. They start breakfast, make lunches, and get everyone out of bed and showered, fed, and dressed. All the time they act as referees and coaches to keep the children from killing one another. They may have to iron something to wear, get ready for work, and think about what to defrost for dinner that evening.

After Mom hustles everyone into the car and off to school, she changes hats and focuses on being a productive professional in the workplace. All attention is on the job for the next eight hours. No mistakes are allowed, and dwelling on her children is taboo. Today's mother must compete in the workplace against men and other women in order to succeed.

At 5 o'clock, she changes hats again and picks up the children from school or the sitter. She has to be patient, attentive, loving, and full of energy. She needs to prepare the evening meal, monitor homework, straighten the house, and offer playtime for the children. Even though Mom's eyelids feel like there are two bowling balls attached to them, she must find that last bit of energy to read a bedtime story, and then war is declared! The children kick, scream, and whine about how underprivileged they are because they have to go to bed. After whips, knives, guns, and chains are used, the little darlings fall asleep. It's now about 8:30.

Mom takes a shower, fixes a glass of tea, and collapses on the couch for some time to herself. She reads a book, balances the checkbook, or stares at TV. Whatever she does, this is her time for enjoyment—fifteen hours after the day began! This cycle is repeated day after day and year after year. Where is her stress level?

Other facts of life for the single mom include thoughts about the present and the future. She may worry about the car falling apart, the checkbook balance, how to pay for health care for her sick child, and whether there will be enough food until payday. She may wonder if she will find a husband in the future or if she even wants another man in her life. Will the child support check be late again? Is she doing a good job raising her children? How is her performance at work? All these things and more she concerns herself with during her private time late at night.

If this woman is married, she must wear one final hat. That is to be a raving beauty queen and a sex maniac for the husband who possibly has been working late, or worse yet has been sleeping in his chair since the four course meal at dinner. If you are a married man with children and do not accept equal responsibility for family chores—shame on you! Your stressors are no more important than your wife's. You should help in all areas, communicate, and show love and concern.

I am not so naive to think that writing your thoughts down will eliminate your stress. This is only one of many techniques I recommend. List all the areas that bother you, why they concern you, and what you can do about each one today. Some people find it helpful to put a goal on the sheet. That is, how you would like things to be. When these major problems are broken apart into little pieces and analyzed, they will appear less frightening. You will have some control. Worrying accomplishes nothing. Writing develops control and gives a sense of direction. Make practical approaches to the problems, and then act. Review the list once a month and update it. When there is nothing you can do about a problem try, to let it go. Go slowly. Be your best friend!

Friendships

Each of us has a circle of friends. I would hope you have one very special friend. It's kind of like a target with various sizes of rings. The outer rings are general acquaintances, and the middle rings are closer friends that you share with; but you've kept the inner circle for that one special friend with whom you can share everything. I believe life is like your children. You get out of it what you put into it. If you take the time to listen and genuinely care for people, the same blessings will be returned. Eventually you will find a friend for life. I am fortunate to have two such individuals.

These people know my hidden secrets and desires. They would support me in any action or decision. I can call on them for a hug, an ear, or a laugh. I feel wanted. I feel important! It is called being connected to life—connected to God.

Stress management involves three entities which should be in harmony. These are body, mind, and spirit. Try to set time aside each week to consciously work on each of these, and before long you will be at peace. You will be calm.

Nutrition

My alma mater, the University of Iowa, completed a ten-year study several years ago to tell us that breakfast is the most important meal of the day. It doesn't sound like much, but eating breakfast is an effective method to combat stress. As with all meals, proper nutrition is essential to our well being.

Without breakfast, we can develop a hypoglycemic reaction by mid-morning. Our fatigue level rises; we become moody, can't concentrate, become dizzy, and develop headaches. We all know the effects of smoking and caffeine. Salt will increase blood pressure. Red meat is very difficult to digest, and our blood is shunted from our muscles to the gut region for digestion when we have a full stomach. Think about how lazy you are after that huge Thanksgiving meal. Red meat at lunch is not as good as fish or a salad if you need to stay awake for that big meeting. I'm not saying not to eat red meat. I'm saying to skip it on those days when your mind and body require you to be alert. Speaking of being alert, raisins are great for stimulating you late in the day. And so is a banana. Have a banana at least for breakfast and even in the middle of the day. It will affect you in a positive way.

Each day we should eat a well balanced diet. We are indeed what we eat. Junk foods and refined sugars are low in nutrition and usually high in calories. If you eat a well balanced diet, you will not usually have to take vitamin supplements. It is also helpful to eat smaller portions but more often. Salt has an attraction for fluid, and eating too much salt will cause your blood pressure to rise, along with your heart rate. Use a salt substitute.

To test your general knowledge of the salt content of foods, I'd like you to take the following test. Arrange these foods from high to low salt content.

Potato Chips	Orange	Pickle
Tuna	Hot Dog	Carrot
Chicken	Pie	Cheese

Here is the correct order from high to low. Pickle (1200mg), tuna (980mg), cheese (700mg), hot dog (550), pie (425mg), potato chips (250mg), chicken (80mg), carrot (30mg), and orange (1mg).

Sugar is another food we consume too much of. Besides being a major cause of tooth decay, increased intake appears to be associated with higher levels of cholesterol and triglycerides. With an excess consumption of sugar, the pancreas releases insulin to reduce the level. As the sugar level drops, so will the energy level, and then the body will release adrenaline. As the adrenaline rises, more insulin is produced to control the blood sugar level. What happens is a constant peak and valley system in which the body doesn't know which way you want it to be. This is physiological stress on the system. To reduce your sugar level:

1. Avoid candies, cakes, and cookies.
2. Don't eat fruits canned in sugar.
3. Avoid heavy doses of honey and syrups, and reduce the use of brown and white sugars.

Many of my patients ask me the best diet or best way to lose weight. I feel the best way to diet is to eat less and exercise more. I always tell them to continue eating a well balanced diet but to reduce the amount of intake. Never should anyone fast as a means of dieting. It is also imperative to exercise while dieting. Did you ever know someone who lost weight only to put it back on in no time at all? We have two types of materials in our bodies. One is fat, and the other is lean tissue. Lean tissue refers to skin, muscle, organs, and bone. If we diet without exercising, we will lose both the lean tissue and the fat. Exercising will reduce the amount of lean tissue loss. It is not the amount of body weight which is important, because some people are naturally big boned or large framed. They may believe they need to lose weight, but their body fat content is fine. The important factor is your percent of body fat, not your weight.

There are various methods of determining body fat. One is called full body immersion, which requires you to be fully submerged in the bottom of a large tank of water and exhale all of your breath. While this is very accurate, these full body tanks are not found in every community. Usually you will find them at major universities. The other problem is that most people don't like this method.

Another method is called the skin caliper test and is quite easy to undergo, but the results are much less accurate. You can find health clubs which may offer this technique. To validate the expertise of the examiner, have him repeat the test on you immediately after he has told you the results. I think you will find quite a difference. I have found the best method to be a measurement through electrical impedance testing. This is very fast, not painful at all, and quite accurate. The cost will range between $15 and $50. This method can be repeated with the same results showing credibility.

Several months ago, I wanted to lose some weight because I was having daily back pain on a regular basis and simply didn't like the way I looked. I began by performing an electrical impedance body fat analysis on myself. My percent of fat was 21%, which was too high, and I needed to lose 23 pounds. I then worked out three times a week for thirty minutes a day on a Nordic Track machine. This machine duplicates cross-country skiing. I also reduced my food intake slightly. In three months, I lost the desired weight, went down two waist sizes and lowered my body fat percentage to 16%. I have not put a single pound back on, feel great, and have no more back pain.

Points to remember

1. Verbal and physical venting are good ways to reduce stress.
2. Writing a letter to someone you are uncomfortable with will help lower stress levels. Say whatever you want. Just don't mail it.
3. Find a close friend; become a good listener.
4. Breakfast is the most important meal of the day. Never skip it!
5. Eat a well balanced diet each day.
6. Reduce your intake of both salt and sugar.
7. The percent of body fat is more important than body weight if you are considering a weight loss program.
8. Always exercise while dieting.
9. Eating less and exercising more is the most sensible way to reduce your weight.
10. Losing two pounds per week is a safe, effective rate.

PART THREE

Reducing Stress at Work

8
Interviewing and Training

By definition, work is a sustained physical or mental effort to overcome obstacles and achieve some objective. To me, this definition has a negative connotation.

Natasha Josefowitz, a reporter representing the Copley News Service, reported in the August 1988, edition of "Business Journal of the Treasure Coast" that half of all managerial activities last less than nine minutes. About 80% of a manager's time is spent in oral communication. She also noted that a study of hospital management found the following to be the most stressful events:
1. Major changes in policies and procedures;
2. Requirements to work more hours than usual;
3. An increase in work pace;
4. A new supervisor;
5. New subordinates;
6. Major reorganization of the department;
7. A change in the nature of the job; and
8. A new co-worker.

The key factors are change or stress. As an employer, I try not to create too many changes at the same time.

If I ever stop having fun at work, I will leave. One priceless treasure I enjoy is that I love my profession and have experienced only a few times of not being excited about going to work. For the first six years of my career, I was under the employ of someone who was not very appreciative, abused my talents, and took me for granted. For the past 13 years, I have worked for a board of directors who treat me completely opposite. I am allowed to blossom and flower into a success, because I am given support, respect, and freedom. I answer to a group of bosses but operate this business as though it were mine. I have their respect.

Starting as a physical therapy aide many years ago, I had the foresight to say several times that if I were able to become a boss I would do things this or that way. Maybe I was destined to become a manager of people one day. Regardless, I am a success. I have fun at work, and I am good at what I do. The most important thing is that I enjoy it. Did you ever stop to think how much time we spend at work versus home? We associate more with our "family" at work than with our real family. There is no way I want to allow unnecessary stress to creep into my work force, and I will do anything to prevent it. I have never fired a single employee. I have had employees who fired themselves. Think about that for a minute. Bosses don't hire someone with plans to terminate them. In my case anyway, all terminated employees did so of their own accord. Some of these created stress for me and after several hours of counseling and after they refused to change, they then terminated themselves—and with my help, of course. We will never have a stress-free work environment. Nor will we ever have a stress-free life. I contend that much of today's stress in the workplace can certainly be reduced significantly to the point where everyone works smarter and harder.

As in my personal life, I can control some of the stressors at work. And I can control all of my reactions to stress at work. In other words, if I have a bad day, it is usually my reaction to a set of circumstances. We each have only ourselves to blame— up to a point! Your boss is not responsible for how you feel. But he may be responsible for that stress which is making you feel that way. He may be the cause. Your mind or attitude is the effect. You can allow his actions to create havoc, or you can adjust and "roll with the punches." The purpose of this section is to give managers better insight into reducing stress on the job. I believe it is managers who are responsible the most for work-related stress. Sometimes employees create problems by negative attitudes or poor performances. That is when they should be dismissed if there is no change after counseling. But it is the bosses who set the tone. They set the pace.

When someone wants to work and wants a job, as all people generally do, there are basic criteria that must be followed and met. You will learn about the interview process, how to train, how to set goals, the use of time management, how to build a team, and the art of communication. The more an employee knows what is expected of him, how he will be evaluated, how he will be rewarded, and how important his role is in the total picture, the better he will perform. An Olympian or any other athlete does not just decide one day to become great. It takes years and years of patience and practice. And it takes years of guidance. If we as managers do not spend time guiding, demonstrating, and teaching, we will never have a workforce of Olympians, and we may be out of a job ourselves. The most valuable asset we have is the people who work with us. Notice I didn't say for us! Our people can make us look good and show the profit we want. They also can ruin our business, no matter how much working capital we have or how important we think we are. Controlling your attitude will help control your stress. This applies at work as well. Maybe, when things go awry, we should look at ourselves first. Remember that when you point a finger at someone else, you have three pointing back at yourself. A new employee is a little like a Little League baseball player. You are his coach, and it's up to you to teach him the rules and techniques of the game. If properly done, the player may just make it to the World Series of Life one day.

Interviewing

So you have 20 people respond to your ad in the classified section on the first day. Hopefully, it's because your business is expanding—not because you fired someone yesterday. Now 20 people respond because you have a "dynamite" company. So what's the first thing you say when your office manager has screened the list of 20 down to 5, based on experience, training, or whatever criteria you told her? Is it, "Oh, I just hate interviewing people. It takes all my energy, and I don't have the time"? I realize you don't have the time. That is our worst enemy in business. But what is more important in your business than the investment you are about to make? And oh, what a great attitude! If you feel this way, it will show; and you are setting the groundwork for future behavior in that new employee.

Make the commitment, set aside plenty of time, and have fun meeting new people. Interview at night after going home to shower and feel refreshed. Can you interview on the weekend? Of course, there is always lunch. The important thing is to make the commitment and allow enough time. The process will be less stressful this way. Did you ever have an interview in which you were shown your work station and introduced to the other employees? And you heard comments like, "Oh, don't worry, we will show you everything. It's no big deal." Not one word was mentioned of the goals, the boss's philosophy, or specific expectations. Interviews such as these are a big joke! That person is no more a manager than a sixth grader. Psychologist Katherine Horney once proposed a theory known as the "Peter Principle." It claims there are times when a person does a fantastic job at a certain level. He is promoted to the next level and fails miserably. There are many bosses who are living examples of the "Peter Principle." They are in their positions not by training, experience, or compassion, but by luck of the draw.

I don't pretend to have all the answers. As a matter of a fact, I never had a single business course in college or grad school. But I can tell you I am successful, I am compassionate, and I care about those around me. Harvard Business School reported that a barometer of a successful organization is reduced employee turnover. I will lose one person every five years from my staff of 13. I have never had an employee quit to work locally in what they thought was a better job. I have had employees who fired themselves, but this only made our organization stronger. In any year we have the potential of having 130 days of sick time used by the total staff, but typically the staff uses about ten days total. My employees enjoy coming to work. What we do works. And if it's not broken, I'm not going to fix it!

My interview process is detailed. After my office manager narrows the list to five applicants, I set aside 45-minute time slots for a second interview. During this stage, I will explain all the general requirements and regulations, along with salary. I will tell them my pet peeves, and my expectations, but mostly I will listen. I want to hear about them and will ask questions like: What does the term "work ethic" mean to you? What did you like least and most about your last job? Why should I hire you? What can you do for my business? I allow them to speak and realize they are very nervous. I remove my white lab coat that is a symbol of authority; I go to the lobby and bring them to my office. I sit next to them and listen! I make no notes but look at them directly and ask them several times if there is anything they want to say before we finish. I treat them as a guest in my home, which is what they are. If they are not chosen for the job, I want them to wish they had been because of my performance and attitude.

I then narrow the list to three people and schedule follow-up interviews. These require 30 minutes each. I review everything that was discussed earlier and present them with a written list of parameters. I give them a tour, introduce them to the staff, and talk more about philosophy and expectations. I do a little more of the talking this time. Each is told I will contact them on a specific day and at a specific time. I already would have notified the other applicants who were rejected.

Before I make my final decision, I do something for myself the night prior to deciding. This might be going to a movie, renting a comedy, or relaxing at the beach. The next morning I shower early, eat a big breakfast, read the paper, and am the first one at work. I then review the three applicants rested and relaxed. Later that morning, I call the one I want and ask if he/she still wants the job. I ask the person to think about it for a few hours and call me back. When he/she returns the call, I establish a set time to begin work and then call the other two who were rejected. These people also receive a thank you letter for applying.

This may sound like a lengthy process. What I have done is to find the attitude I want around me. That person comes to work already feeling like part of the team. He/she is still nervous, as we all were the first day; but they join my team on the run. I think it is wiser to spend more time with the investment at the beginning than to rush through a process only to err and have to spend more time counseling and documenting—not to mention fighting possible litigation. This person will make my life easier, and I want to be sure all parties will be happy.

Training

The easy part is over. Now it's time to get to the business of business. Where it all starts and where it's most important is the training. I allow at least 45 minutes the first day to spend one-on-one with my new employee. I review all expectations and have them sign documents they understand and in which they agree to follow my rules. Never assume the person knows a thing. That way you will never overlook any area. Take them through a step-by-step process regarding what to do and how to do it, from the time they drive onto the property. I will assign another employee to take this person under their wing during training. I delegate this responsibility and spend countless hours explaining what I want done and how. In essence, I train two people simultaneously. My employee who assists with the training receives additional pay for the added responsibility. We have the new person spend the day getting acquainted with the business, the surroundings, and the people. I would never give someone a job to do the first day. We start by having them read our 300-page manual and review the business goals (which I will explain later). The goal of training is to capitalize on their enthusiasm and to make them feel special and wanted. Even when someone has been with me for years, I want them to feel wanted and special. Because they are!

We start slowly learning general things, such as equipment and where supplies are located, and then have the person observe. I meet again with the person at noon and then at day's end. I ask these guestions: What did you see that you wonder about? What did you like about your first day? What did you not like? To make a new employee feel special, never allow him to go to lunch alone that first day. Plan a staff lunch or ask co-workers to take that person to lunch with them. Buy a coffee cup or another small gift as a welcome present the first day. Plan a staff meeting. One thing on the agenda would be to ask several staff members to tell the new person some things about themselves and their job role. Again, your role the first day is to make your new employee feel proud and pleased that he took this job. Remember, you want the employee to always feel this way.

I can never over-educate my patients or my staff. The more everyone knows, the better for me, as I will have less stress and can enjoy my work much more. Consequently, I provide copies of the manual, job description, names/addresses of employees, hierarchy of authority, philosophy, goals, and anything else I find pertinent. I want them to go home not wondering if they made the right decision. I want them to be filled with excitement about working with me.

After one to two full days of observing, I then begin very slowly the hands-on training. I have seen people become overwhelmed with duties because too much was thrown at them too soon. Your employees are your ambassadors. They are an extension of you—a reflection of you. If you err by throwing the new person into action before they are ready, business will suffer, you will be stressed, and your new employee will be stressed also.

By week's end, this person will know the general operation of my business, will understand safety, and will have learned a few procedures, know the staff, and feel comfortable. I try to have new employees begin with me in the middle of the week. Remember the last time you started a new job with all the anxiety and stress. It is very fatiguing, and my goal is to keep them calm as they learn.

An attitude I have that has helped me to stay successful is that no single person is any better than any other. And I do not tolerate someone pretending to be better or belittling a fellow employee. We are all part of a family, and everyone is equal. There is no job beneath me. That is why I always say that a person works with me, not for me.

Points to remember

1. Try to have fun at work.
2. My attitude about problems determines my stress level.
3. The more information an employee has, the better he will perform.
4. The most important asset in a business is the employee.
5. Devoting ample time to the interview process can save you plenty of headaches in the future.
6. All employees should always feel proud to work with you.
7. Training should proceed slowly, and communication should be at its highest point.
8. No single employee is better than any other employee.

9
Evaluations/Rewards/ Job Description

The employee knows how to do his job. He has been trained. There is more to being an effective employee than just going through the required motions. Characteristics such as attitude, initiative, hustle, cooperation, promptness, and teamwork are also very important. Now, I would be remiss in my duties if I did not share with my employees the exact characteristic of what makes a valued employee. People are not mind readers. As an employee, you should ask specifically what the boss wants out of you in terms of performance. As an employer, you should educate the employees concerning your expectations. The more information there is, the less stress there will be. Do this in private and in open meetings. Then guide the employees. When was the last time any of us went to the boss and asked how we were doing? Believe me, it's okay. By doing this you also show that you care about your performance.

I believe in honest, open communication. It's not fair when bosses hold things in all year and then at promotion time say, "Well, there are many things you did this year that irritated me." This is called "gunny-sacking." It is an unfair practice that is done frequently. I follow the Golden Rule and ask myself how I would like it if that were done to me.

I evaluate or consult with new employees weekly for the first month, then once a month for the next three. All employees are evaluated twice a year. At the halfway point, we review their performance and establish areas that need work for the second half of the year. I tell them that if all their personal growth areas are met, they will be amply rewarded if it's financially feasible. There is never a guarantee of an automatic pay raise. We are all in this together. We sink or swim together. Everyone wins, or no one does.

My midterm and annual performance reviews are in written form, and each person receives a copy and signs a paper that he was reviewed and received a copy. My goal is to be fair. To do so sometimes requires me to say things that may hurt other people. Honesty is sometimes painful at first but alleviates unwanted stress in the future. All my employees know exactly where they stand at any given moment and what they need to do for improvement.

The employer's rights are to state and maintain standards, expect cooperation and participation, and obtain a commitment to improve. The employer's responsibilities are to define job requirements, communicate goals and requirements clearly, and appraise performance in a fair way.

The employee's rights are to receive adequate training and support, have expectations clearly defined, and receive a fair evaluation. The employee's responsibilities are to meet all standards, cooperate, and participate in the company, and correct unsatisfactory performance. Again referring to that Little League player—he cannot successfully play second base if he has never received proper training and does not know what is expected of him.

Every business should have written goals. Each year I provide a copy to employees. There are times when I will post them throughout the year as a reminder. The single most important factor in the success of any business is the goal the owner wants to achieve. It may be as simple as, "I want to make a profit." Training should then be given on what each person needs to do on a personal level to meet your goals. People are not mind readers. Bosses should show each person what to do. Some require less time than others to understand and hence receive more money than others. Be specific with explanations. Compliment their work. Delegate responsibility and then monitor but do not constantly oversee it. Let it go. Everyone wants to succeed; if you provide the guidance and support, most people will. Delegating minor jobs reduces your workload and your stress and gives the employee a sense of control over his destiny and reduces his stress.

Each person should have a specific job description, and it should be updated annually. I tell my employees that I want them to write theirs (after they have been with me for several years), and to write it in such a way that if they died tomorrow a new person could pick it up and be able to follow it with no problems. Be specific! Heard that before?

With goals and job descriptions in hand, the performance review is ready to begin. I don't want any barriers when I am communicating with people. Each person knows we will be evaluating, so he/she may prepare, just as I do. I do not wear typical "boss clothes" but instead wear blue jeans or plain slacks and an open shirt. I would not wear my white lab coat, tie, etc. I do not want any symbol of authority. I'm after honest communication. I don't meet in my office but in a neutral area and allow ample time for the evaluation. The occasion when I meet in my office and have every symbol of authority at my disposal is when I'm going to reprimand someone. Then I am not their guidance counselor, but then I am the boss! When I finish, the point will have been made.

In today's work world, documentation is the key to preventing unwanted court appearances. You can never overdocument. If you are honest, there will be nothing to hide. Give employees copies of everything in their folders. Have no surprises. Shoot from the hip. I evaluate from specific areas. These include: standards and policies, patient care, relationship with co-workers, and goal analysis. In each section, I develop what is important to me and have a rating scale from 1-4 representing "never" to "always." You can make one easily.

I also have a list of questions related to the job itself. These include: Do you know what is expected of you? Do you get enough help in improving your performance? What problems do you have and what are your solutions? How could your job be improved? Do you think all requirements are fair and reasonable? What are your personal and business goals for the next six months?

After our discussion, I tell them this was a dry run and the evaluation that counts will be in six months, prior to their annual raise. In six months, I use the semi-annual review as a guide for their performance. Those who met the goals and improved their performance based on the previous critique are rewarded. When there is no improvement, there's no increase. If there still is no change at the next review, then they have terminated themselves. Everyone is responsible for his destiny and actions. These are the rules of the game.

This type of evaluation lets all concerned know where they stand and helps to reduce stress. Once a year I have the employees evaluate me through a questionnaire and this is done anonymously. They circle 1-5 that represents "strongly disagree" to "strongly agree" on a list of about twenty questions I have developed. This way I can assess if I am communicating all areas of the business appropriately.

When an employee pleases me for what he has done, I will single him out and shout from the highest mountain how proud I am. I will call him into a board meeting and tell the entire board of directors, will compliment him at a staff meeting, and send him a written note of thanks for his special attitude. I believe we should hire by attitude, not necessarily by credentials. I prefer a new employee with no experience and a big heart, to an employee with all kinds of experience but no human relations skills. Fewer problems. Less stress!

If an employee needs reprimanding, this is done in the privacy of my office. It's no one else's business what is said. It stays there; and once I have said my piece, the issue is essentially dead. I will remember what transpires and expect a correction. If there is no change, I meet again; and the tone is more harsh and everything is documented, signed, and a copy given to the employee. This way that person can never say I did not inform them of a deficiency. Again, I am providing information.

There are certain ways to reward people without costing a great deal. Give a gift certificate for a massage, a nice meal, a trip to the beauty shop, a dozen golf balls, etc. Give the person a day off with pay. Place a small ad in the classified section to say thanks. Whatever you choose, be sincere and do it right after the event. It will mean more. A great tool I use is to write the person a note to say how much I enjoy working with him. I am a firm believer in "what goes around comes around."

Office morale

When the office stress is low, productivity is high. When you manage by allowing people to have control over their destiny, by delegating and group problem solving, a very cohesive and tight-knit organization will develop. Teamwork will be high. When employees know their suggestions will be heard and when you are a good listener, your staff will do anything for you. We have a rule of letting someone know if you had a bad night or are down in the dumps. When an employee tells me he is having a bad day, I will not give him any new projects and will give an added amount of TLC. We all protect each other. I don't care to know what the details are. I just want to know if it's an off day. If he doesn't tell me, I might assume a poor attitude is developing. As an employee, I would encourage you to communicate with your supervisor. Tell him/her up front that you are having a bad time. Communication and information are key words for a stressless office.

All employees and employers would be better off by consciously trying some of the following: Set priorities. Use time management. Learn coping skills. Learn to take criticism and believe you can make a difference. Develop a loving, lasting relationship. Learn to appreciate nature. Ask yourself if what you do really matters. Realize that your worth as a person is not tied to your efforts at work. Talk about your feelings with those with whom you have a conflict. Give in periodically. Take one little piece at a time, and the puzzle will take care of itself. Do something for others, but don't tell anyone you did it. Give up the super-urge person. Go easy with criticism of others. Give the other person a break. Remember that what you give to others, you give to yourself. Let others win sometimes. Learn to accept what you cannot change. Balance work with recreation. Saying you "choose to" rather than you "have to" makes you less of a victim and feel more in control. Do the most difficult or boring task at your best time of day, when you're full of energy. Go for short walks in the office to burn off stress. Take lunch out of the building. Say "no" when you can't take on more. Mentally escape for short periods. Talk with your supervisor about problems. And get off the pity pot. Don't be a martyr.

The following applies to either the home or the office: Remove your glasses to give your eyes a rest. Focus out the window briefly. Stand periodically and stretch. Surround yourself with happy, positive people. Listen to "peppy" music when fatigued and "mellow" music when hyper. Take fifteen two-minute breaks rather than two fifteen-minute breaks. Take cat naps at lunch. Read books dealing with your hobbies at lunch. Give yourself a small treat because you have earned it. Go slowly. Stop being critical of yourself. Rather than being your worst enemy, learn to be your best friend!

Once a year we draw names for our secret pals. Each employee is responsible for his secret pal on holidays and birthdays, and for special attention when that person is down. We buy small gifts and cards, or just send a note in the mail to let him know someone cares.

Points to remember

1. Bosses should give plenty of information to employees. You can never give too much.
2. When an employee knows exactly what is expected, he will perform better, and there will be less stress.
3. Evaluations twice a year with goal setting are both helpful way to reduce stress.
4. Any business should have written goals and a job manual which covers every possible aspect of the business.
5. There are certain rights and responsibilities for both the employer and the employee.
6. Delegation is one way to reduce stress and workload.
7. Every person needs a specific job description.
8. Praise in public, and criticize in private.
9. Learn to say thanks to your employees.

PART FOUR

Retirement and Stress

10

Problems with Retirement

Does your back go out more than you do? Is that sweet little old lady you are helping across the street your wife? Are your golden years covered with ten karat gold instead of twenty-four karat? Do you ever wonder who ever coined the term goldenyears? Welcome to the life of retirement! As Jackie Gleason used to say, "How sweet it is!" Or is it?

I instruct senior citizens in my stress classes and find a unique set of concerns and problems. Their test scores on the Major Lifestyle Test are usually low, and yet they too have stress. I smile as the younger members wonder what possible stress the older folks could have. Your homes are paid for, you no longer work, you have a nestegg, your children are gone, and you have plenty of time. There appears to me to be four categories of major stress factors with seniors. Please excuse me if I am presumptuous, as I am not yet retired. All I can draw on is 18 years of observation as a physical therapist. What I see daily includes the following concerns: Reduced self-esteem, finances, health, and personal mortality.

I live in a small retirement city in Florida where the average age is about 52. Sixty percent of my patients are over the age of 65. Most all are living the American Dream of retiring and residing in Florida. I hope the people in Arizona don't get upset with me for that comment. These retirees come from all walks of life and economic classes. Most of them grew up in the Depression and still prefer Benny Goodman to the Beatles. They believe, as you, do that in America you should give a hard day's work for a day's pay— and then you will be amply rewarded and live "happily ever after."

No one prepared you in your 40s and 50s, while you were working, for the changes that now confront you. That nestegg seems so small compared to your original expectations because of inflation. Do you feel bored with nothing to do? Do you sometimes feel unwanted or unproductive? Do waves of sadness pass over you like a cloud? Do you feel lonely and think about your death? These things and more are what I hear from my patients.

Common concerns of retirees who uproot and move to another state include: No close ties with the family, lifelong friends are "back home," you miss your grandchildren, finding new friends is difficult, and living in a retirement facility, i.e., condominium or mobile home park, is different than expected.

What did you expect during retirement? Did you plan and set goals for these years? Or did you just roll along, taking what was offered? The stress techniques mentioned in earlier sections will work for you. There are other things you can do to help yourself that are unique to your age group.

Health concerns

It is such a shame that retirees work so hard and follow all the rules, only to have a catastrophic illness and lose all financial security because of medical bills. The concern for health and finances go hand in hand. And rightly so! I see women bringing their husbands in for treatment after strokes, Parkinson's, or other debilitating illnesses. Many of these women know very little about financial matters or how to read an insurance policy; some can't drive; others feel abandoned by their spouse. All are frightened because of the unknown and are alone because their families are in another state. They have few people to turn to for help. Through it these women hold up remarkably well. When her husband dies, the wife's health often worsens. This is due possibly because of sustained stress on her. She then develops her own illnesses.

Another situation I see even more is the unrealistic expectations many senior citizens have regarding their health. I say this not in a negative way but strictly as an observation of a health care professional. Many of my patients forget the body wears out and want me to make them young again. That will not happen, no matter how much you want it. You can learn through proper instruction how to make adjustments for that back pain or arthritis. You can find alternate activities to replace the more vigorous ones you have been doing for years. A physical therapist can guide you as to proper exercises, body mechanics, and general health tips and hints. But neither your therapist nor your doctor can make you young again. You should set goals and then discuss them with qualified individuals to see if they are realistic.

One of my patients had a mild stroke with very little paralysis. His entire life revolved around golf. This was something he would never play again. He had no other hobbies or interests and went into a deep state of depression. He refused to exercise or participate in his therapy program. He refused counseling. His life consists of feeling sorry for himself as he does nothing except watch TV. His wife calls me periodically for advice because he won't leave the house, won't shave, but just sits. He could be on a walking or swimming program. He could be bicycling or traveling. Instead, he chooses to let life pass him by. Do you have varied interests? Are you locked into one favorite activity? Start today to find new interests! They may come in handy.

Remember when your children were young and you were concerned who their friends were? You didn't want any bad influences on your children. Did you ever hear, "You are who you hang around with"? When I was in college, I was involved in athletics. Doing well in sports was more important to me than grades. All my friends were athletes, and we just didn't study that much. In my junior year of undergraduate school, I decided I wanted to become a therapist; to do so required a change in study habits. So, I began to hang around with premed, chemistry, and psychology majors who were concerned about their performances in the classroom. My habits and my grades changed. I became like those I associated with.

Peer pressure has no age limit. It is with you now during retirement. Look at your friends. Are they whiners and complainers? Do they only talk about their medical problems? Do you find yourself leaving the party feeling drained or frustrated? Negative thinking and behavior can rub off on each of us if we allow it. It can bring you down and make you feel depressed.

The other day at lunch, a large group of seniors sat next to our table. Each talked at the same time, and each talked only of their aches and pains! Not one person listened to the others. One of my patients told me she enjoys her bridge game every week, as it is her main social function. It seems one lady lost her husband six months ago, and all she does is talk about it. The other women lost their husbands a long time ago; and each finds it frustrating, because the conversation is always the same. No one wants to say anything, because they don't want to appear calloused. So they sit there grinding their teeth. I suggested that someone tactfully say the conversation should not center on any negative subject. If any member of the group slips, then a fine of a dollar should be levied. Each week the money could be given to a charity. It could be a fun way to refocus the conversation and reduce the stress. I refuse to be around negative people who only see clouds. That is another option for you to consider.

Finances

Our society designs financial help when people become indigent. God forbid you might have some savings to hold you over for that rainy day and then become ill. You will receive no assistance until all resources exhaust themselves. To make matters worse, inflation erodes your investments; and then try to work at gainful employment and live off what the tax structure allows retirees to earn. Financial problems can ruin a young marriage, strap the middle age, and be devastating to the elderly.

Some of my patients eat only one meal a day. They are frugal shoppers by necessity. Many cannot afford to run their air conditioners, so they swelter in the summer heat. Imagine what nutrition one small meal a day provides. As they become indigent, food stamps and rent subsidy may become available. There are a few health care facilities, such as the one I work in, that offer free medical care to the needy. I see pride take over where logic ought to prevail. Some of my patients absolutely refuse free service. They believe in the American dream and the "system." Accepting charity is beyond their comprehension.

I suggest they evaluate their expectations. Joining a support group to hear how others cope can be helpful. If there is none in your community, start one at your church or synagogue. Throw away credit cards. Buy nothing on time. Talk with your accountant or find a good financial advisor to assist you. Establish a budget, and follow it.

A tragedy I read about every year is how older people get scammed by some con artist in Florida. It must occur in other states; but because I live here, I see it reported on local news. A naive retiree will withdraw all his savings and give the cash to a supposed law enforcement agent. This "agent" is checking on a bank employee suspected of embezzlement. The "agent" will mark the cash and then return the money to the retiree, who will re-deposit it. The con man disappears, and the person is out all his savings. Other scams include a free roof inspection. After problems are detected, a large deposit is required for the repair. Again, the con man skips with all the cash. No one offers something for nothing. Be suspecting of free gifts or services. Always investigate people or businesses before allowing them to work for you. Ask to see their occupational license and proof of insurance. Imagine what would happen if you hired a handy man through the classified ads and he has no insurance. Who do you suppose will pay if he injures himself on your property? In my business I see patients who are called symptom magnifiers, more commonly known as fakers. These individuals will complain of pain and other vague symptoms until their lawsuit settles. Then they miraculously become better. These people live in every city in America. Beware! You could become a victim.

A falsehood that many retirees live under involves Medicare and Social Security. When the bill became law, it was not the intent that Social Security become a retirement policy. It is supplemental and is not designed to be your sole source of income. Having Medicare does not entitle you to receive free medical care.

Every month new regulations and restrictions are developed by the bureaucrats. These are designed to keep the program funded and to keep everyone confused. I think these Federal employees lie awake at night imagining what they can do next to confuse us further. This way they will have a job in the future. I love my profession and my patients. My feelings toward Medicare are at the other end of the spectrum. Because this program is so confusing, older folks have a difficult time understanding how to file a supplemental claim, and many will ask what they owe. Hospitals give free seminars on a range of topics. Call your local hospital and ask the marketing director to provide a seminar on Medicare. Have them teach you how to read EOBs, how Medicare works, and and any other topics you want. Please don't tell them I suggested it, or I will start receiving hate mail! AARP could also be a valuable forum for guest speakers speaking on the subject of Medicare. The more you learn, the less frustrated you will be.

Mortality

This is a very personal area that is no major problem for some people and is a source of fright for others. Each of us must face our own mortality in our own way. I see sadness come over the faces of my patients when they tell me another friend died. It is not only the loss of a friend but the realization that time is limited. This fact will not go away; and if you dwell on it, you can affect the quality of your future years.

I see people develop depression because of their thoughts on mortality. It can become a vicious cycle making you susceptible to drug or alcohol abuse. I read somewhere there are more drug addicts on prescriptions than on the streets. I have seen suicides because of these people dwelling on their mortality. I see the elderly give up and become sick or develop a death wish to "get it over."

One answer is your heart and soul. If things are right with your higher power, and you have a kind heart and settled mind, this burden may be lightened. Talk to your clergy or your friends, or join a support group. The important thing is to realize you are not alone. You are not crazy. This is a common feeling; and when you discuss feelings, calm will prevail. Be kind to yourself!

Self-worth

Self-worth or self-esteem is important to everyone regardless of age. A negative self value can create havoc on a small child or a 98-year-old senior. Sitting on the pity pot can be a difficult habit to break and can lead to further low esteem. I suggest you read the previous chapter again on this topic.

I hear patients say their usefulness to society has diminished and they are bored with nothing to do. A wife may say her husband is driving her nuts, because he putters around the house all day and either doesn't do a thing or complains all the time. Is this you?

Do you feel that you are not a productive part of society? Do you feel there are no challenges in your life? I see married people who say that when the children leave they will do things together. This desire keeps getting pushed back further every year so that when they retire problems result. There are then two strangers living in the same house with different dreams and different expectations. Begin today to regroup. Talk to your mate and set goals. Find mutual interests and different interests. Share yourself and you inner feelings. These are not the days of Audie Murphy and John Wayne. It is okay for men to cry and to share their inner selves. The days of stuffing your feelings are long gone. Shed a tear, and you will feel a lot better. And you will still have that precious male ego! After you realize it's normal to feel the way you do, a new life can begin.

A mind is indeed a terrible thing to waste. I believe that if you don't use it, you'll lose it. Tax and test yourself. Get away from that stupid idiot box. Sell it at a yard sale and start reading or communicating. Do something for others. Giving money to a charity through your fraternal organization is not what I mean. That's too easy! Actually do something for someone. Volunteering with a school, Little League, church, non-profit facility, or any other group will make you feel better. In my community, there is a group named RSVP. This is an acronym for Retired Senior Volunteer Program. Senior citizens volunteer their expertise to any group. If you were in public relations, you might want to write a newsletter for some group. A retired carpenter would be helpful to anyone. A teacher could help others to read. Whatever you did when you were working you can do now. Just because your business said it was time to stop doesn't mean you have to quit everything. I believe the debt we owe to God is payable to mankind. You were blessed to have a trade or profession, and now is the grand time to repay society. And guess what! While you are helping your fellow man, you will feel like a million bucks. Your self-esteem will rise, and you will rest better at night.

One of my best friends is the ultimate example of how to retire. Neal is in his late 60s and retired from Southern Bell Telephone. He tells me that his first thought upon retiring was that a load was lifted from him. He then felt he was wasting time doing nothing. He set out to develop two areas that provide productive time and consequent self-worth. His productive time entails woodworking. Some things he would sell, and others he gave away. Then he enrolled in junior college and graduated with a 3.85 grade average. Neal is still excited about how he was accepted by young students.

Where some retirees take on public service, Neal finds enjoyment in his hobbies. These include the following: flying radio controlled airplanes, playing golf, operating a HAM radio, making stained glass projects, working on his computer, shooting at a gun club, gem cutting, walking, and running his toy train. He also is an avid reader and loves to learn new card and board games. He was a Navy photographer and donates his talents to schools and nonprofits when they need such services. He does not have time to get bored or feel sorry for himself.

Points to remember
1. Set specific retirement goals and write a plan to achieve those goals.
2. Develop a wide list of varied interests and hobbies.
3. Associate only with a positive, upbeat circle of friends.

4. Join a support group for retirees.
5. Investigate businesses prior to hiring them for work on your home, yard, car, etc.
6. Social Security should not be your only means of retirement—it is a supplement.
7. Share feelings about death with others.
8. Get involved in your community by volunteering.

11
Solutions to Retirement Stress

Besides the solutions I mentioned earlier, there are some things unique to both sexes and to you as a couple. My solutions are in no way meant to degrade either sex. These are based solely on my observations.

If you are a woman who does not know how to drive, I would suggest you learn in all weather conditions. Ask someone to teach you how to make minor repairs around the house and on the car. It will save you money and frustration in the future. I would give you my wife's number, but she is already too busy making the repairs on our house for me. She teaches me all I need to know about mechanical things. Please learn to read a map if you don't know how. My mother did not even know how to take a city bus or how to drive. When my Dad died, she was dependent on others for all her transportation. Do you know how to start the lawn mower? If you are not the one who pays the bills, now is the time to learn. Get instruction in setting up a general ledger and journal. Banks will help you pay your bills and will charge you as well. Do you know where all important papers are if needed in an emergency? Do you know where those insurance papers are and how to read them?

Now for the poor, little, helpless creatures we call men! Learn to cook. Ask your wife how to wash and dry clothes and how to iron without ruining the equipment. You should learn basic sewing such as how to sew on a button. If you do not pay the bills, ask your wife to show you what to do. When is the last time you cleaned the house? And please learn how to dress. Don't depend on your wife for all the answers. Be observant in what she recommends. Try dressing yourself, and go to the mall. If people are snickering and pointing, you failed the dress test. Try again! Seriously though, I tell both of you these simple things to eliminate stress in the future when one of you becomes sick or dies.

It is important to have a will and specific instructions in the event of death. Thousands of dollars can be spent needlessly when we are emotionally distraught. Have all preparations made ahead. My wife knows all the details I want at my funeral from the location of my ashes to the songs. When I die, she needs to give my written instructions to a friend who will help with the arrangements. It will reduce her stress.

Stress affects all ages, and retired seniors have some special needs. Choose what you want from this book, and leave the rest. Go slowly and be kind to yourself. The answers to peace of mind are in your heart. Seek, and you will find!